W9-DGT-129

Carnegie Commission on Higher Education
Sponsored Research Studies

CENTERS OF LEARNING:
BRITAIN, FRANCE, GERMANY,
UNITED STATES
Joseph Ben-David

BLACK ELITE:
THE NEW MARKET FOR HIGHLY
EDUCATED BLACK AMERICANS
Richard B. Freeman

PH.D.'S AND THE
ACADEMIC LABOR MARKET
Allan M. Cartter

DEMAND AND SUPPLY
IN U.S. HIGHER EDUCATION
*Roy Radner and
Leonard S. Miller*

FACULTY BARGAINING:
CHANGE AND CONFLICT
*Joseph W. Garbarino and
Bill Aussieker*

COMPUTERS AND THE
LEARNING PROCESS IN
HIGHER EDUCATION
*John Fralick Rockart and
Michael S. Scott Morton*

WOMEN AND THE POWER TO CHANGE
Florence Howe (ed.)

THE USEFUL ARTS AND
THE LIBERAL TRADITION
Earl F. Cheit

TEACHERS AND STUDENTS:
ASPECTS OF AMERICAN
HIGHER EDUCATION
Martin Trow (ed.)

THE DIVIDED ACADEMY:
PROFESSORS AND
POLITICS
*Everett Carll Ladd, Jr.
and Seymour Martin Lipset*

EDUCATION AND POLITICS
AT HARVARD
*Seymour Martin Lipset
and David Riesman*

HIGHER EDUCATION AND EARNINGS:
COLLEGE AS AN INVESTMENT AND A
SCREENING DEVICE
Paul Taubman and Terence Wales

EDUCATION, INCOME, AND HUMAN
BEHAVIOR
F. Thomas Juster (ed.)

AMERICAN LEARNED SOCIETIES
IN TRANSITION:
THE IMPACT OF DISSENT
AND RECESSION
*Harland G. Bloland and
Sue M. Bloland*

ANTIBIAS REGULATION
OF UNIVERSITIES
Richard A. Lester

CHANGES IN UNIVERSITY
ORGANIZATION, 1964–1971
Edward Gross and Paul V. Grambsch

ESCAPE FROM THE DOLL'S HOUSE:
WOMEN IN GRADUATE AND PROFESSIONAL
SCHOOL EDUCATION
Saul D. Feldman

HIGHER EDUCATION AND
THE LABOR MARKET
Margaret S. Gordon (ed.)

THE ACADEMIC MELTING POT:
CATHOLICS AND JEWS IN
AMERICAN HIGHER EDUCATION
Stephen Steinberg

LEADERSHIP AND AMBIGUITY:
THE AMERICAN COLLEGE
PRESIDENT
*Michael D. Cohen and
James G. March*

THE ACADEMIC SYSTEM IN
AMERICAN SOCIETY
Alain Touraine

EDUCATION FOR THE PROFESSIONS OF
MEDICINE, LAW, THEOLOGY, AND SOCIAL
WELFARE
*Everett C. Hughes, Barrie Thorne,
Agostino DeBaggis, Arnold Gurin,
and David Williams*

THE FUTURE OF HIGHER
EDUCATION:
SOME SPECULATIONS AND
SUGGESTIONS
Alexander M. Mood

CONTENT AND CONTEXT:
ESSAYS ON COLLEGE EDUCATION
Carl Kaysen (ed.)

THE RISE OF THE ARTS ON THE AMERICAN
CAMPUS
Jack Morrison

THE UNIVERSITY AND THE CITY:
EIGHT CASES OF INVOLVEMENT
George Nash, Dan Waldorf, and Robert E. Price

THE BEGINNING OF THE FUTURE:
A HISTORICAL APPROACH TO GRADUATE
EDUCATION IN THE ARTS AND SCIENCES
Richard J. Storr

ACADEMIC TRANSFORMATION:
SEVENTEEN INSTITUTIONS UNDER PRESSURE
David Riesman and Verne A. Stadtman (eds.)

WHERE COLLEGES ARE AND WHO ATTENDS:
EFFECTS OF ACCESSIBILITY ON COLLEGE
ATTENDANCE
*C. Arnold Anderson, Mary Jean Bowman, and
Vincent Tinto*

NEW DIRECTIONS IN LEGAL EDUCATION
*Herbert L. Packer and Thomas Ehrlich
abridged and unabridged editions*

THE UNIVERSITY AS AN ORGANIZATION
James A. Perkins (ed.)

THE EMERGING TECHNOLOGY:
INSTRUCTIONAL USES OF THE COMPUTER IN
HIGHER EDUCATION
Roger E. Levien

A STATISTICAL PORTRAIT OF HIGHER
EDUCATION
Seymour E. Harris

THE HOME OF SCIENCE:
THE ROLE OF THE UNIVERSITY
Dael Wolfle

EDUCATION AND EVANGELISM:
A PROFILE OF PROTESTANT COLLEGES
C. Robert Pace

PROFESSIONAL EDUCATION:
SOME NEW DIRECTIONS
Edgar H. Schein

THE NONPROFIT RESEARCH INSTITUTE:
ITS ORIGIN, OPERATION, PROBLEMS, AND
PROSPECTS
Harold Orlans

THE INVISIBLE COLLEGES:
A PROFILE OF SMALL, PRIVATE COLLEGES
WITH LIMITED RESOURCES
Alexander W. Astin and Calvin B. T. Lee

AMERICAN HIGHER EDUCATION:
DIRECTIONS OLD AND NEW
Joseph Ben-David
(Out of print, but available in
paperback from the University of Chicago Press.)

A DEGREE AND WHAT ELSE?
CORRELATES AND CONSEQUENCES OF A
COLLEGE EDUCATION
Stephen B. Withey, Jo Anne Coble, Gerald Gurin,
John P. Robinson, Burkhard Strumpel, Elizabeth
Keogh Taylor, and Arthur C. Wolfe

THE MULTICAMPUS UNIVERSITY:
A STUDY OF ACADEMIC GOVERNANCE
Eugene C. Lee and Frank M. Bowen

INSTITUTIONS IN TRANSITION:
A PROFILE OF CHANGE IN HIGHER
EDUCATION
(INCORPORATING THE 1970 STATISTICAL
REPORT)
Harold L. Hodgkinson

EFFICIENCY IN LIBERAL EDUCATION:
A STUDY OF COMPARATIVE INSTRUCTIONAL
COSTS FOR DIFFERENT WAYS OF ORGANIZING
TEACHING-LEARNING IN A LIBERAL ARTS
COLLEGE
Howard R. Bowen and Gordon K. Douglass

CREDIT FOR COLLEGE:
PUBLIC POLICY FOR STUDENT LOANS
Robert W. Hartman

MODELS AND MAVERICKS:
A PROFILE OF PRIVATE LIBERAL ARTS
COLLEGES
Morris T. Keeton

BETWEEN TWO WORLDS:
A PROFILE OF NEGRO HIGHER EDUCATION
Frank Bowles and Frank A. DeCosta

BREAKING THE ACCESS BARRIERS:
A PROFILE OF TWO-YEAR COLLEGES
Leland L. Medsker and Dale Tillery

ANY PERSON, ANY STUDY:
AN ESSAY ON HIGHER EDUCATION IN THE
UNITED STATES
Eric Ashby

THE NEW DEPRESSION IN HIGHER
EDUCATION:
A STUDY OF FINANCIAL CONDITIONS AT 41
COLLEGES AND UNIVERSITIES
Earl F. Cheit

FINANCING MEDICAL EDUCATION:
AN ANALYSIS OF ALTERNATIVE POLICIES AND
MECHANISMS
Rashi Fein and Gerald I. Weber
(Out of print, but available from University Microfilms.)

HIGHER EDUCATION IN NINE COUNTRIES:
A COMPARATIVE STUDY OF COLLEGES AND
UNIVERSITIES ABROAD
Barbara B. Burn, Philip G. Altbach, Clark Kerr,
and James A. Perkins

BRIDGES TO UNDERSTANDING:
INTERNATIONAL PROGRAMS OF AMERICAN
COLLEGES AND UNIVERSITIES
Irwin T. Sanders and Jennifer C. Ward

GRADUATE AND PROFESSIONAL EDUCATION,
1980:
A SURVEY OF INSTITUTIONAL PLANS
Lewis B. Mayhew
(Out of print, but available from University Microfilms.)

THE AMERICAN COLLEGE AND AMERICAN CULTURE: SOCIALIZATION AS A FUNCTION OF HIGHER EDUCATION
Oscar Handlin and Mary F. Handlin

RECENT ALUMNI AND HIGHER EDUCATION: A SURVEY OF COLLEGE GRADUATES
Joe L. Spaeth and Andrew M. Greeley
(Out of print, but available from University Microfilms.)

CHANGE IN EDUCATIONAL POLICY: SELF-STUDIES IN SELECTED COLLEGES AND UNIVERSITIES
Dwight R. Ladd
(Out of print, but available from University Microfilms.)

STATE OFFICIALS AND HIGHER EDUCATION: A SURVEY OF THE OPINIONS AND EXPECTATIONS OF POLICY MAKERS IN NINE STATES
Heinz Eulau and Harold Quinley
(Out of print, but available from University Microfilms.)

ACADEMIC DEGREE STRUCTURES, INNOVATIVE APPROACHES: PRINCIPLES OF REFORM IN DEGREE STRUCTURES IN THE UNITED STATES
Stephen H. Spurr

COLLEGES OF THE FORGOTTEN AMERICANS: A PROFILE OF STATE COLLEGES AND REGIONAL UNIVERSITIES
E. Alden Dunham

FROM BACKWATER TO MAINSTREAM: A PROFILE OF CATHOLIC HIGHER EDUCATION
Andrew M. Greeley

THE ECONOMICS OF THE MAJOR PRIVATE UNIVERSITIES
William G. Bowen
(Out of print, but available from University Microfilms.)

THE FINANCE OF HIGHER EDUCATION
Howard R. Bowen
(Out of print, but available from University Microfilms.)

ALTERNATIVE METHODS OF FEDERAL FUNDING FOR HIGHER EDUCATION
Ron Wolk
(Out of print, but available from University Microfilms.)

INVENTORY OF CURRENT RESEARCH ON HIGHER EDUCATION 1968
Dale M. Heckman and Warren Bryan Martin
(Out of print, but available from University Microfilms.)

The following technical reports are available from the Carnegie Commission on Higher Education, 2150 Shattuck Ave., Berkeley, California 94704.

RESOURCE USE IN HIGHER EDUCATION: TRENDS IN OUTPUT AND INPUTS, 1930–1967
June O'Neill

MAY 1970: THE CAMPUS AFTERMATH OF CAMBODIA AND KENT STATE
Richard E. Peterson and John A. Bilorusky

MENTAL ABILITY AND HIGHER EDUCATIONAL ATTAINMENT IN THE 20TH CENTURY
Paul Taubman and Terence Wales

AMERICAN COLLEGE AND UNIVERSITY ENROLLMENT TRENDS IN 1971
Richard E. Peterson

PAPERS ON EFFICIENCY IN THE MANAGEMENT OF HIGHER EDUCATION
Alexander M. Mood, Colin Bell, Lawrence Bogard, Helen Brownlee, and Joseph McCloskey

AN INVENTORY OF ACADEMIC INNOVATION AND REFORM
Ann Heiss

ESTIMATING THE RETURNS TO EDUCATION: A DISAGGREGATED APPROACH
Richard S. Eckaus

SOURCES OF FUNDS TO COLLEGES AND UNIVERSITIES
June O'Neill

TRENDS AND PROJECTIONS OF PHYSICIANS IN
THE UNITED STATES 1967–2002
Mark S. Blumberg

THE NEW DEPRESSION IN HIGHER EDUCATION
—TWO YEARS LATER
Earl F. Cheit

PROFESSORS, UNIONS, AND AMERICAN
HIGHER EDUCATION
Everett Carll Ladd, Jr. and
Seymour Martin Lipset

A CLASSIFICATION OF INSTITUTIONS
OF HIGHER EDUCATION

POLITICAL IDEOLOGIES OF
GRADUATE STUDENTS:
CRYSTALLIZATION, CONSISTENCY, AND
CONTEXTUAL EFFECT
Margaret Fay and Jeff Weintraub

FLYING A LEARNING CENTER:
DESIGN AND COSTS OF AN OFF-CAMPUS SPACE
FOR LEARNING
Thomas J. Karwin

THE DEMISE OF DIVERSITY?:
A COMPARATIVE PROFILE OF EIGHT TYPES OF
INSTITUTIONS
C. Robert Pace

TUITION: A SUPPLEMENTAL STATEMENT TO
THE REPORT OF THE CARNEGIE COMMISSION
ON HIGHER EDUCATION ON "WHO PAYS?
WHO BENEFITS? WHO SHOULD PAY?"

THE GREAT AMERICAN DEGREE MACHINE
Douglas L. Adkins

AN OWL BEFORE DUSK
Michio Nagai

DEMAND AND·SUPPLY IN UNITED
STATES HIGHER EDUCATION:
A TECHNICAL SUPPLEMENT
Leonard A. Miller and Roy Radner

The following reprints are available from the Carnegie Commission on Higher Education, 2150 Shattuck Ave., Berkeley, California 94704.

ACCELERATED PROGRAMS OF MEDICAL EDUCATION, by Mark S. Blumberg, reprinted from JOURNAL OF MEDICAL EDUCATION, vol. 46, no. 8, August 1971.*

SCIENTIFIC MANPOWER FOR 1970–1985, by Allan M. Cartter, reprinted from SCIENCE, vol. 172, no. 3979, pp. 132–140, April 9, 1971.*

A NEW METHOD OF MEASURING STATES' HIGHER EDUCATION BURDEN, by Neil Timm, reprinted from THE JOURNAL OF HIGHER EDUCATION, vol. 42, no. 1, pp. 27–33, January 1971.*

REGENT WATCHING, by Earl F. Cheit, reprinted from AGB REPORTS, vol. 13, no. 6, pp. 4–13, March 1971.*

COLLEGE GENERATIONS—FROM THE 1930s TO THE 1960s, by Seymour M. Lipset and Everett C. Ladd, Jr., reprinted from THE PUBLIC INTEREST, no. 25, Summer 1971.*

WHAT'S BUGGING THE STUDENTS?, by Kenneth Keniston, reprinted from EDUCATIONAL RECORD, American Council on Education, Washington, D.C., Spring 1970.*

*The Commission's stock of this reprint has been exhausted.

THE POLITICS OF ACADEMIA, by Seymour Martin Lipset, reprinted from David C. Nichols (ed.), PERSPECTIVES ON CAMPUS TENSIONS: PAPERS PREPARED FOR THE SPECIAL COMMITTEE ON CAMPUS TENSIONS, American Council on Education, Washington, D.C., September 1970.*

INTERNATIONAL PROGRAMS OF U.S. COLLEGES AND UNIVERSITIES: PRIORITIES FOR THE SEVENTIES, by James A. Perkins, reprinted by permission of the International Council for Educational Development, Occasional Paper no. 1, July 1971.*

FACULTY UNIONISM: FROM THEORY TO PRACTICE, by Joseph W. Garbarino, reprinted from INDUSTRIAL RELATIONS, vol. 11, no. 1, pp. 1–17, February 1972.*

MORE FOR LESS: HIGHER EDUCATION'S NEW PRIORITY, by Virginia B. Smith, reprinted from UNIVERSAL HIGHER EDUCATION: COSTS AND BENEFITS, American Council on Education, Washington, D.C., 1971.*

ACADEMIA AND POLITICS IN AMERICA, by Seymour M. Lipset, reprinted from Thomas J. Nossiter (ed.), IMAGINATION AND PRECISION IN THE SOCIAL SCIENCES, pp. 211–289, Faber and Faber, London, 1972.*

POLITICS OF ACADEMIC NATURAL SCIENTISTS AND ENGINEERS, by Everett C. Ladd, Jr., and Seymour M. Lipset, reprinted from SCIENCE, vol. 176, no. 4039, pp. 1091–1100, June 9, 1972.

THE INTELLECTUAL AS CRITIC AND REBEL, WITH SPECIAL REFERENCE TO THE UNITED STATES AND THE SOVIET UNION, by Seymour M. Lipset and Richard B. Dobson, reprinted from DAEDALUS, vol. 101, no. 3, pp. 137–198, Summer 1972.

THE POLITICS OF AMERICAN SOCIOLOGISTS, by Seymour M. Lipset and Everett C. Ladd, Jr., reprinted from THE AMERICAN JOURNAL OF SOCIOLOGY, vol. 78, no. 1, July 1972.

THE DISTRIBUTION OF ACADEMIC TENURE IN AMERICAN HIGHER EDUCATION, by Martin Trow, reprinted from THE TENURE DEBATE, Bardwell Smith (ed.), Jossey-Bass, San Francisco, 1972.

THE NATURE AND ORIGINS OF THE CARNEGIE COMMISSION ON HIGHER EDUCATION, by Alan Pifer, based on a speech delivered to the Pennsylvania Association of Colleges and Universities, Oct. 16, 1972, reprinted by permission of the Carnegie Foundation for the Advancement of Teaching.

AMERICAN SOCIAL SCIENTISTS AND THE GROWTH OF CAMPUS POLITICAL ACTIVISM IN THE 1960s, by Everett C. Ladd, Jr., and Seymour M. Lipset, reprinted from SOCIAL SCIENCES INFORMATION, vol. 10, no. 2, April 1971.*

THE POLITICS OF AMERICAN POLITICAL SCIENTISTS, by Everett C. Ladd, Jr., and Seymour M. Lipset, reprinted from PS, vol. 4, no. 2, Spring 1971.*

THE DIVIDED PROFESSORIATE, by Seymour M. Lipset and Everett C. Ladd, Jr., reprinted from CHANGE, vol. 3, no. 3, pp. 54–60, May 1971.*

*The Commission's stock of this reprint has been exhausted.

JEWISH ACADEMICS IN THE UNITED STATES: THEIR ACHIEVEMENTS, CULTURE AND POLITICS, by Seymour M. Lipset and Everett C. Ladd, Jr., reprinted from AMERICAN JEWISH YEAR BOOK, 1971.*

THE UNHOLY ALLIANCE AGAINST THE CAMPUS, by Kenneth Keniston and Michael Lerner, reprinted from NEW YORK TIMES MAGAZINE, November 8, 1970.*

PRECARIOUS PROFESSORS: NEW PATTERNS OF REPRESENTATION, by Joseph W. Garbarino, reprinted from INDUSTRIAL RELATIONS, vol. 10, no. 1, February 1971.*

. . . AND WHAT PROFESSORS THINK: ABOUT STUDENT PROTEST AND MANNERS, MORALS, POLITICS, AND CHAOS ON THE CAMPUS, by Seymour Martin Lipset and Everett C. Ladd, Jr., reprinted from PSYCHOLOGY TODAY, November 1970.*

DEMAND AND SUPPLY IN U.S. HIGHER EDUCATION: A PROGRESS REPORT, by Roy Radner and Leonard S. Miller, reprinted from AMERICAN ECONOMIC REVIEW, May 1970.*

RESOURCES FOR HIGHER EDUCATION: AN ECONOMIST'S VIEW, by Theodore W. Schultz, reprinted from JOURNAL OF POLITICAL ECONOMY, vol. 76, no. 3, University of Chicago, May/June 1968.*

INDUSTRIAL RELATIONS AND UNIVERSITY RELATIONS, by Clark Kerr, reprinted from PROCEEDINGS OF THE 21ST ANNUAL WINTER MEETING OF THE INDUSTRIAL RELATIONS RESEARCH ASSOCIATION, pp. 15–25.*

NEW CHALLENGES TO THE COLLEGE AND UNIVERSITY, by Clark Kerr, reprinted from Kermit Gordon (ed.), AGENDA FOR THE NATION, The Brookings Institution, Washington, D.C., 1968.*

PRESIDENTIAL DISCONTENT, by Clark Kerr, reprinted from David C. Nichols (ed.), PERSPECTIVES ON CAMPUS TENSIONS: PAPERS PREPARED FOR THE SPECIAL COMMITTEE ON CAMPUS TENSIONS, American Council on Education, Washington, D.C., September 1970.*

STUDENT PROTEST—AN INSTITUTIONAL AND NATIONAL PROFILE, by Harold Hodgkinson, reprinted from THE RECORD, vol. 71, no. 4, May 1970.*

COMING OF MIDDLE AGE IN HIGHER EDUCATION, by Earl F. Cheit, address delivered to American Association of State Colleges and Universities and National Association of State Universities and Land-Grant Colleges, Nov. 13, 1972.

MEASURING FACULTY UNIONISM: QUANTITY AND QUALITY, by Bill Aussieker and J. W. Garbarino, reprinted from INDUSTRIAL RELATIONS, vol. 12, no. 2, May 1973.

PROBLEMS IN THE TRANSITION FROM ELITE TO MASS HIGHER EDUCATION, by Martin Trow, paper prepared for a conference on mass higher education sponsored by the Organization for Economic Co-operation and Development, June 1973.*

*The Commission's stock of this reprint has been exhausted.

Centers of Learning

BRITAIN, FRANCE,

GERMANY, UNITED STATES

by *Joseph Ben-David*

Professor of Sociology
The Hebrew University of Jerusalem

An Essay Prepared for
The Carnegie Commission on Higher Education

MC GRAW–HILL BOOK COMPANY
New York St. Louis San Francisco
Auckland Bogotá Düsseldorf Johannesburg
London Madrid Mexico Montreal
New Delhi Panama Paris São Paulo
Singapore Sydney Tokyo Toronto

The Carnegie Commission on Higher Education,
2150 Shattuck Avenue, Berkeley, California 94704,
has sponsored preparation of this essay as
part of a continuing effort to obtain and present
significant information for public discussion.
The views expressed are those of the author.
Part of this research was supported by a Ford
Foundation grant and carried out at the
University of Chicago.

CENTERS OF LEARNING

Britain, France, Germany, United States

This book was set in Palatino by University Graphics, Inc.
It was printed and bound by The Maple Press Company.
The designer was Elliot Epstein. The editors were Nancy Frank
and Cheryl L. Hanks for McGraw-Hill Book Company and
Verne A. Stadtman and Karen Seriguchi for the Carnegie Commission
on Higher Education. Audre Hanneman edited the index. Milton J. Heiberg
supervised the production.

Library of Congress Cataloging in Publication Data

Ben-David, Joseph
Centers of learning.

Bibliography: p.
Includes index.
1. Education, Higher—United States. 2. Education,
Higher—Great Britain. 3. Education, Higher—France.
4. Education, Higher—Germany. I. Carnegie Commission
on Higher Education. II. Title.
LA173.B46   378   76-45798
ISBN 0-07-010133-7

123456789MAMM76543210987

Contents

Foreword

When the Carnegie Commission on Higher Education wanted someone to make a study of the comparative effectiveness of different national systems of higher education, Joseph Ben-David was a natural choice. His unusually clear perceptions of American higher education were evident in another book in the Commission's series entitled *American Higher Education: Directions Old and New*, which has been well received by serious students of higher education here and abroad. His knowledge of other national systems of higher education is equally prodigious, having been acquired by both firsthand experience and careful scholarship. It is fortunate for all of us that he found time during busy and, at times, trying years to accept the Commission's invitation to make the study that yielded this book.

Those who would expect a study of comparative effectiveness to produce quantitative measurements of national investments and outcomes related to higher education should be aware from the beginning that the author has not taken that approach. Nor has he attempted to gather comparative data from a large number of countries. He has, instead, chosen to concentrate on four countries with systems of higher education that have had visible influence beyond their national boundaries. By treating these systems historically, he demonstrates, first of all, that the effectiveness of higher education systems is closely related to the social, economic, and political contexts within which they develop. But even more fundamentally, he shows that effectiveness is related to the functions of the systems.

The stage for Professor Ben-David's essay is set by reminding us that the reforms of Western systems of higher education in the seventeenth and eighteenth centuries centered, to a considerable extent, on efforts to break down the monopolies the ancient learned professions had held in institutions of higher learning. The reforms had surprisingly different results in France, Germany, and England, if one sees only their impacts on the profession of academics. But they did succeed in extending the prestige and benefits of higher learning to new professions. And it is in professional education that higher education is found by Professor Ben-David to be most successful today.

Other functions are less well served. General education, which never was well developed in continental Europe but once was regarded as a particularly strong function in the United States, is held to be of continuing importance but in trouble everywhere. Research, which Ben-David finds to have an intriguingly different character in each of the major learning centers he describes, now suffers from its slackening ties to general education and its inability to sustain itself solely within the confines of universities. The function of political criticism is seen less as a frightening newcomer than as a function once taken for granted and unobtrusively served—and carefully controlled. In the absence of such controls in the future, this function will always have the potential of seriously disrupting institutions of higher learning, causing disaffection between institutions and society and undermining needed financial support. Professor Ben-David also sees the functions of furthering social justice and equality as continuing rather than new. Problems with this function may have more to do with ill-reasoned solutions than with the function itself.

By making a historical study of national higher education endeavors, Professor Ben-David helps us to avoid the consternation that might set in if we were to view universities only in the context of their current problems and inadequacies. Remedies are possible, and some are suggested by the author. They may not all enjoy quick acceptance. Some of them are sure to generate controversy. Improvements will not come easily, but they can be made by slow, careful effort. And this is an appropriately optimistic note with which to leave readers of this final publication in the Carnegie Commission's series on higher education.

Clark Kerr
Chairman
Carnegie Commission
on Higher Education

November 1976

Centers of Learning

1. *Introduction*

Never before had higher education expanded as rapidly and universally as it did in the 1960s.[1] University education in the industrially developed countries grew at annual rates ranging from 4.2 to 16.2 percent between 1960 and 1965.[2] Growth continued throughout the sixties (Ushiogi, 1971, p. 351), coming to a sudden halt about 1970 (Carnegie Commission, 1971, pp. 2–3; Freeman & Breneman, 1974, pp. 3, 14). Change for the worse was exacerbated by the student revolts of 1968 and after, followed by the worst economic depression of the post-World War II period. These events undermined public confidence in man's ability to solve social and economic problems by rational, scientific means—a confidence on which so much of the support of higher education depends—and caused an inevitable reduction in university incomes. This extreme swing of fortunes led to a widespread and deep-seated malaise in the academic world.

The reaction of the intellectual community to this unexpected change of fortunes has been a typical case of *anomie* ("normlessness"), a concept coined by Emile Durkheim to describe the disorientation caused by unexpected social change, such as the ups and downs of the business cycle (Durkheim, 1951, pp. 241–276). The disorientation is caused, according to Durkheim, by one's tendency to project existing trends into the future. Near the peak or the trough of business cycles, people lose their standards of judgment. When business grows rapidly for a

---

[1] Except, of course, during periods following the establishment of new or drastically reformed systems of higher education.

[2] The only exception was Yugoslavia, whose rate was 1.3. This, however, was compensation for an extremely high annual growth rate of 11.9 percent during the previous five years (Organisation for Economic Co-operation and Development, 1971, p. 44).

while, people become overoptimistic and borrow and invest, until they find themselves bankrupt. When business contracts, they do the opposite, with similarly disastrous results. Of course, not everyone falls victim to such disasters. Probably a majority preserve their prudence, or at least their luck. But the feeling of disorientation and of an absence of norms and reasonable expectations affects everyone.

There is such a state of disorientation in higher education today. The rapid growth of demand for university training and research of the late fifties and early sixties led to rosy forecasts of insatiable needs for new graduates, and to a belief in a new alchemy capable of turning knowledge into gold or, at least, anything that gold can buy.[3] This optimistic outlook was promptly reversed when, at the end of the sixties, university expansion began to slow down and student activism disturbed the tranquility of academic life. There emerged new prophecies about the decline of Western science, as well as of the so-called elitist higher education (that is, of higher education aimed at the acquisition of individual competence) in general (Blanpied, 1974; Roszak, 1974). Even those of us who did not accept these prophecies were faced—at least temporarily—with a declining demand for higher education and scientific research and low scientific morale unrelieved by exciting new discoveries.

During the last two years the acute crisis came to an end. With few exceptions, academic work at universities is back to normal. There is still no solution to the economic plight of higher education, but even in this respect there has been some stabilization in most countries, and the situation does not appear as hopeless as two or three years ago. But there has been no rebirth of optimism, and no resumption of constructive initiative. The doubts and uncertainties about the future of higher learning and research have not been dissipated. They only appear as less threatening than in the early seventies, because we have grown so accustomed to them that we barely notice them. The disorientation still prevails, hope for little

---

[3]"Society is supporting this structure [of science] and paying for it more and more because the results of [the scientist's] work are vital for the strength, security, and public welfare of all. With everything said to be depending on him, from freedom from military attack to freedom from disease, the scientist now holds the purse-strings of the state" (Price, 1963, p. 111). See also Bell (1968, p. 198), and Denison (1962).

more than academic survival counts as optimism, and few people dream of significant advances.

This mildly depressed state of academic morale threatens to become chronic, and time alone—without human effort—will not cure it. It is, therefore, important to try to see things in a perspective unaffected, as far as possible, by the prevailing mood. In order to avoid seeing the present malaise as the sole determinant of everything expected in the future, an attempt will be made to view the principal systems of higher education in the Western world as historical entities, namely, to see in response to what needs they first emerged, how they developed their structures, and how they responded to changing needs and opportunities. It is hoped that this will provide a useful perspective for viewing the state of higher education today as a stage in a continuous development, with ups and downs, rather than as an abrupt, perhaps final, crisis.

It must be emphasized, however, that this perspective will not provide a basis sufficient for predicting the future. Even if it were possible completely to explain the past and present states of higher education, it would still be impossible to predict its future. Social institutions are open systems, and no one can know whether their future will be determined by the same variables that determined their past and present. One circumstance in particular makes forecasts impossible. Up until now, modern higher education has developed almost exclusively in Europe and North America. Higher education elsewhere has been largely an imitation of European and American models, and there is still no serious challenge to European-American leadership in higher learning.[4]

One of the most important characteristics of these models has been the principle of "academic freedom," according to which higher learning and research have to be free from political, religious, and ideological control. This principle had been undermined by extremist groups and academic freedom was abolished permanently or temporarily in all the countries of

---

[4]This is not to say that this leadership is always happily accepted. In different parts of the world there are attempts to assert the cultural independence of universities from the European-American centers. But so far these attempts have been mainly ideological and have produced no systems of higher education capable of standing scientifically on their own feet (see Foster, 1975; Yesufu, 1973).

continental Europe—except Sweden and Switzerland—by communist, fascist, and nazi regimes or occupation between the nineteen twenties and the nineteen forties. The only academically central countries in which the principle of academic freedom has been consistently preserved are Britain and the United States.[5] The importance of these countries in the world of learning ensured the survival of the belief in the principle even in countries in which academic freedom was not officially respected. This has been an important condition of the preservation of some unity of purpose, interests, and norms of conduct in higher education everywhere. Even in countries in which everything is subject to the State, there is much de facto independence of the system of higher education.

However, all this may drastically change. Even in Britain and the United States, universities are more dependent on the State these days than ever before, which means that their ability to take an independent stand on political and ideological issues is at least potentially threatened. Furthermore, the world environment is more inimical to academic freedom today than it has been for the last hundred years or so. In most parts of the world universities are under strict political control, and teachers and students have little or no freedom to voice opinions of their own. International cultural organizations, such as UNESCO (United Nations Educational, Scientific, and Cultural Organization), are ruled by governments for whom political considerations override any concern for scientific truth (Hoggart, 1975), and even international learned societies are under pressure to submit to the demands of governments disrespectful of the autonomy of science.[6]

These processes have made deep inroads in the institutional autonomy of universities and leave them open to a variety of external influences, making generalizations and predictions based on the experience of the past even more difficult than before. Therefore, the main contribution of sociological analy-

---

[5]This is not to say that there have been no infringements of freedom in these countries. Some of these, especially those initiated by the late Senator McCarthy in the nineteen forties and early fifties, were quite serious. But these infringements never led to the abolishment of the principle.

[6]An example of this is the custom of electing officers of international scientific associations to represent various political blocs. In the social sciences this arrangement is actually used for making political propaganda at international meetings (see Worthington, 1975).

sis to the determination of the future is not in predicting trends, but in enlightening decisions. Better understanding of the past and the present exposes unexpected consequences of past actions, latent functions of existing arrangements, and relationships between structures and functions that usually go unnoticed. This should be of some help in deciding what is worth preserving and what is not. To serve as an aid in such decisions is the purpose of the analyses undertaken in this book.

THE SCOPE OF THE INQUIRY A book on higher education in the entire world would be an undertaking beyond the powers of the author. However, the systems to be discussed in this book—those of England, France, Germany, and the United States—are not just an arbitrary collection, but are the central part of the world system. There are large and important systems of higher education in China, India, Japan, and the Soviet Union, and some smaller systems are also important. But so far, none of these systems has had much influence outside the boundaries of these states or areas controlled by them politically. In contrast, the French, German, and American systems (in this order) have, in turn, served as centers and models for world higher education, with England as a durable secondary center, since the beginning of the nineteenth century (Ashby, 1966; Shils, 1966; Ben-David, 1971, pp. 19–20; Yuasa, 1974). They became centers of learning because they developed a high degree of all-around scientific excellence and self-sufficiency over a long period of time. It is difficult to imagine what science would be like today if, say, Italy, Sweden, or Switzerland had been the only countries cultivating science during the last 200 years. But Britain, France, Germany, and the United States could each have developed modern science in about the same way as it has actually developed, although, of course, at a slower pace.[7] Other indexes of the self-sufficiency of these countries are the extent to which it is possible to write textbooks or build a high-level introductory course by using local publications as primary sources, or to train people locally on an advanced level in the most important fields of science and scholarship.

This is not to say that research in these countries has been on

---

[7]For the United States this is true only for the last hundred years. Until the 1870s, the United States was a scientifically peripheral country.

a higher level than in the smaller or peripheral countries. Some of these later, such as the Netherlands, Sweden, and Switzerland, have had excellent higher education. But their excellence was to a large extent dependent on the openness of their systems toward the centers. Thus the excellence of the university and the ETH (*Eidgenössische Technische Hochschule,* somewhat freely translated as the Federal Institute of Technology) in Zurich was to a large extent the result of the ability of these institutions to attract able young scholars from Germany who had the potential to become leaders in their fields, but who still had to make their reputations before receiving an offer from one of the more centrally located German-language universities, such as Berlin, Munich, Leipzig, or Vienna (Gagliardi, 1938, p. 552; Zloczower, 1966, p. 47). Dutch and Scandinavian universities have been able to maintain their excellence by the cosmopolitanism of their scholars, who almost invariably speak excellent English, German, and very often also French, and who have been able to maintain close contacts with the world centers through study and work abroad. Scholars in these countries were extremely quick to change their orientation from Germany to England and the United States in the 1930s, when Germany lost its leading place in science. At that time, in a crucial field of science, theoretical physics, Copenhagen even became a world center for a brief period.

Similar tactics have been followed by some of the newer scientific communities of recently developed or still-developing countries, such as Iran, Israel, Japan, and Turkey. Those peripheral countries that for political or linguistic reasons have been slower to follow the shift of centers have been doing more poorly than the ones capable of quick shifts or lucky enough to be attached to a thriving center. Thus, Belgium and Switzerland both suffered scientifically—compared to the Netherlands and the Scandinavian countries—as a result of their continued allegiance to the German and French centers even in periods of weakness in the latter. India and other former British dependencies have done better scientifically than former French dependencies, probably because of the greater scientific strength of the British center and its close linguistic relationship to the American one. And Arabic- and Spanish-speaking countries have probably suffered in their scientific development by the fact that they constitute large enough cultural areas to make their scholars reluctant to attach themselves to a foreign center, yet have not been able, so far, to develop scientific centers of their own. Japan, of course, is potentially in the same position, and the tendency to parochialism is indeed extremely strong among Japanese scholars. But it has been counteracted by deliberate policies of the Japanese government and, immediately after the Second World War, by the American occupation.

Studying these differences in the strategies of peripheral countries would be a fascinating subject, but something quite different from studying the systems of the scientifically central countries. It seems justified to devote a book entirely to the latter countries, for even though this will be only part of the story, it will be an important part of it with a coherent meaning of its own.

2. Modern Higher Education: Its Emergence and Structure

In all literate societies there have been institutions of higher education to cultivate and transmit intellectual tradition at its highest level. The Academy of Plato, the Lyceum of Aristotle, and the higher schools in China, India, and among Arabs and Jews all educated advanced students who went to study with teachers famous for their knowledge and originality of thought. Much of what was done in these institutions of learning was similar to what is done today. If they suddenly appeared among us, Plato, Aristotle, or Euclid could, within reasonable time, probably catch up with present-day developments and be employed as professors at any university. Therefore, when speaking of modern higher education one runs into a difficulty similar to that encountered by Max Weber and others when they tried to speak about modern capitalism. Higher education, capitalism, and many other social institutions developed over a long period of time, and their development cannot be broken into precise stages.

Nevertheless, the present system of higher education—which many believe is on its way out—has certain characteristics that distinguish it from previous systems. These are its emphasis on specialization and the openness of the traditions it cultivates. The notion of general, or liberal, education still exists today, and many students in the United States—though nowhere else—study for a liberal arts degree. However, the liberal arts curriculum is not uniform, but is a combination of more or less specialized courses that have little or nothing in common except the student who studies them. Moreover, this vague liberal arts tradition is recognized only at the first degree level. All the higher degrees are specialized, and they are all supposed to impart to the student some specialized knowledge and skill that can be utilized—at least in principle—in some professional activity. This last includes degrees in the basic arts and sciences that qualify their holders to teach.

This system contrasts sharply with higher educational practices in non-European civilizations and even with European practices prior to the nineteenth century. Although much discussion of specialized practical higher education took place in eighteenth-century Europe, actual experiments of this kind were few and not systematically executed. The Scottish and some continental European universities improved their medical teaching (which also included chemistry), and there was much advocacy of, and a few experiments in, the creation of engineering schools of a fairly advanced level, such as the *Ecole nationale des ponts et chaussées* in France, or the *Bergakademie* in Freiberg, Germany. But until the end of the eighteenth century, higher education was overwhelmingly education in the classical languages and in the reading and interpretation of classical texts. Exceptions were the Scottish and one or two reformed German universities that introduced modern subjects and taught almost everything in the vernacular, rather than in Latin, but even in those universities there was very little specialization and research (Paulsen, 1921, pp. 109–113, 126–148; Taton, 1964, pp. 18–23, 179–184; Sloan, 1971, pp. 23–32).

The only specialized studies at the universities were in law, theology, and medicine, and even those were not very specialized. It was important, of course, for a theologian to know Greek and Latin, and for a lawyer to know Latin. Both benefited from mastering the techniques of correct textual interpretation, since their jobs were, in part, based on that. But there is no reason to believe that a physician capable of reading Galen in the original was a better practitioner than one who acquired his medical knowledge through apprenticeship. Even specialists trained in modern scientific and technical studies, such as the French and German experiments in engineering education, were not better than the apprenticeship-trained engineers in England (Béland, n.d.).

Indeed the purpose of higher education—including education for the professions—was not to train students for a variety of specialties but to transmit the intellectual heritage. This is not to say that education was not practical. In many ways it was more practical than it is today, because being learned was a sign of unusual ability that conferred on the person honors and occupational advantages, especially in the so-called learned professions of law, medicine, and theology. These advantages were justified by the belief that the learned were intelligent and that learning imparted wisdom, skills, and habits of thinking that could be used in everything a person did. There was no assumption, however, that one could apply theoretical learning directly to technical problems, except to some extent in law. Of course, one could apply one's learning directly as a teacher, but teaching in itself was not a respected profession. Only teachers who had high status in the professions of law, theology, and medicine were really respected. The kind of higher education in which a person studies a specific subject with the expectation of making a respectable living out of practicing that subject was, by and large, an innovation of the nineteenth century, although the idea of such an education had existed in the eighteenth century and even before.

Another innovation of the nineteenth century was what has been referred to above as the openness of the traditions cultivated at the universities. Science and scholarship were assumed to be continuously advancing, and higher education had to keep pace with this advancement. In most cases this implied that the university was engaged in both research and teaching. In this respect too, no hard and fast distinction can be made between modern and earlier types of higher education. Leading intellectuals, usually the preeminent teachers in institutions of higher education, were always supposed to make original contributions to learning, to discover contradictions in existing traditions, and to solve them. Occasionally these scholars were capable of viewing a tradition as a whole and of discovering its internal logic and systematizing it in a new, more efficient way, resolving in the process many of its problems. The transformation into systems of the Talmudic tradition by Maimonides in the twelfth century and of the Christian theological tradition by Thomas Aquinas in the thirteenth century were such scientific feats. And in the eighteenth century many university professors, such as Haller in Bern, Boerhave in Leiden, and Black in Edinburgh, did research in empirical science.

But the idea that universities transform disciplines or split them into specialties, or that they may develop entirely new disciplines, or combine different ones in order to create an intellectual capacity for the solution of practical problems, emerged only in the nineteenth and twentieth centuries in the course of programmatically pursued research at universities.

THE MOVEMENT TOWARD MODERN SYSTEMS
Those who initiated the modernization of higher education in France, Germany, and England were philosophers, scholars, and administrators. Administrators were least important in England; instead, an ill-defined group of professional people, some businessmen, and public figures played a role in the movement. There was such a group in France, too, but its members were less important than they were in England. Everywhere these initiators of modernization were dissatisfied with the increasing gap between the classical education given at the universities and the new scientific research and the modern literary-philosophic culture that grew up outside the universities. They considered unjust the occupational privileges of the university-educated in professional work, education, and administration, partly because they considered classical education irrelevant for most of this work, and partly because university education was usually of poor quality. They believed that a more modern and scientific education would be more practical as well as more democratic than the prevailing one. There was a strong belief in the applicability of science, especially to medicine and engineering, and selecting the administrative elite through an education that conferred specific technical qualification in fields relevant to their work seemed to be more equitable than selecting them according to university degrees testifying to some general learning of doubtful relevance to the task. This is not to say that classical education was not appreciated. But it was felt that its dominant place in higher education was exaggerated and that the privileged position of the universities was unjustified on both intellectual and utilitarian grounds.

The purpose of the reformers everywhere throughout the eighteenth century and until about 1810 was to create specialized professional schools instead of university faculties. Innovations in what can be broadly referred to as higher education consisted in most cases of the establishment of specialized professional schools outside the universities, such as the previously mentioned engineering schools and the schools for officers in the technical branches of the military, or of the creation of professorships in science outside the universities, such as the science professorships at the *Collège de France* (before the Revolution, *Collége des lecteurs royaux*) or the *Musée d'Histoire naturelle* (then *Jardin du roi*) in Paris (Carr-Saunders & Wilson, 1933; Hahn, 1971, pp. 185–193; Hans, 1951, pp. 209–219; König, 1970, pp. 22–29). There were similar specialized institutions in the German *Länder* (states) for engineering and medical education. In England there were private proprietary schools in medicine, and the training for such important professions as law and engineering was transmitted through private apprenticeships. These institutions seemed to be the logical result of the criticism leveled against the universities. They were specialized, utilitarian, and free of inherited privilege. And they could accommodate as teachers the scientists who at that time could not find a place in the universities. Berthollet and Fourcroy, for example, lectured at the *Jardin du roi* and Laplace taught at the *Ecole militaire* prior to the Revolution (Crosland, 1967, pp. 98, 102).

The intellectual circles that initiated the ideas of reform did not act in a social vacuum. Low-grade professionals, such as technologists, apothecaries, pharmacists, and the like, envied the privileges of the old learned professions and also had a vital interest in the reforms. In France these groups were not well organized and had no positive policies of their own. They were instrumental in closing the universities and academies in 1793, but left the establishment of new institutions in the hands of intellectuals and civil servants. On the other hand, in England, which had a stronger tradition of corporate action by interest groups, the upcoming lower professional groups played an important role in the reforms.

In Germany or, more precisely, in Prussia, which had been the intellectually and—next to Austria—the politically leading German state at the end of the eighteenth century, the situation was quite different. Throughout the eighteenth century the Prussian ruling classes followed the French Enlightenment. They showed little favor to the traditional universities and were inclined to replace them by practically oriented professional schools. As has been pointed out, some schools of this kind were established toward the end of the eighteenth century. These reforms would also probably have been acceptable to the lower professional classes had they had a say in the matter, and some of them, such as the pharmacists, had established proprietary schools of their own.

However, the decisive class in Germany, even more than in France, was the intellectuals. But this was a class different from its counterparts in France and England. In the latter countries the intellectuals were part of thriving bourgeois classes, and many of them belonged to the upper classes. In France they often shared the same views as the upper civil servants, and some of the latter were intellectuals themselves.

In Prussia, and elsewhere in Germany, the intellectuals usually came from more modest backgrounds. Many of them were sons of clergymen (who had lower status in Germany than in England). Due to the growing spirit of secularism, intellectuals no longer entered the clergy as others like them had done before. They interested themselves in the broad field of learning and methodical thinking, which was then called philosophy, and in literature. They were seeking social recognition and, above all, a safe income—both of which were very much out of their reach. The bourgeoisie was relatively poor and backward, the aristocracy had no tradition of education, and the minority who had such interests preferred French to German education. There were few attractive careers in the professions, the civil service, and teaching, and, apparently, much less scope for the free-lance writer-intellectual than in England or France (Brunschwig, 1974, pp. 119–163). University appointments offered among the most attractive careers, but the universities were traditional institutions, dominated by the professional faculties of law, theology, and medicine, and did not allow real freedom of thought and speech, since they were subject to the control of both the state and the church. Partly because of this control, universities were also intellectually poor institutions.

This dissatisfaction with the universities should have made the German intellectuals open to the Enlightenment idea of replacing the universities with professional schools. But this idea was preempted by the upper bureaucrats who preferred French to German culture, and science to philosophical and literary erudition. Specialized professional schools had little demand for philosophers and humanists. Therefore the German movement of intellectuals was equally opposed to the new specialized professional schools and the old universities (König, 1970, pp. 65–97, 102–107).

The initiative to reform higher education in the United States began much later than in Europe, and it was much more directly influenced by the example of a single foreign country, Germany, than the European reforms. Therefore, one can treat the American reform as an extension of the reforms in Europe, while the reforms in the major European countries were, in spite of mutual influences, relatively more determined by local traditions and internal social forces. Therefore I shall first deal with the European countries and subsequently with the American case.

THE NEW SYSTEMS
The arbiter to which the conflicting groups addressed themselves everywhere—with the partial exception of England— was the government, which had the authority to change the system of higher education. But the roles the governments of these three countries played in the reform of higher education differed greatly.

In France, the reform movement tried to use the government as its patron from the very outset. For centuries there had been a continuing feud between a centralizing civil service and the professional guilds, including the church-dominated universities, which represented particularistic social values. Civil servants were not unsympathetic to the reformers, and, on many occasions, adopted policies advocated by them even during the old regime. But during the old regime these reforms were cautious and partial, because although the civil service usually sympathized with reform in principle, the regime was committed to upholding traditional privileges.

The obstacles to complete reform were removed by the Revolution. In 1793 the universities were abolished along with all the other institutions of the old regime. The new system that began to emerge in 1794 consisted of a series of professional schools for teachers, doctors, and engineers needed by the state. Scientific studies and scientistic philosophy were to inherit the central place that had been occupied by the classics in both secondary and higher education (Liard, 1888, pp. 255–311).

Eventually, under Napoleon, the scientific orientation was

weakened, the emphasis on the new scientistic philosophy was completely abolished, and classical learning was restored to its former importance in secondary schooling. But higher education remained identified with specialized education for various professions. The professional schools for medicine and law were now called faculties. These were not parts of a university, but separate institutions that belonged to the general educational system (the "university" in the peculiar Napoleonic terminology). In addition, there were central professional schools, *grandes écoles*, to train the elite engineers and teachers for the advanced classes of the lycées and for higher education, and *écoles des applications* to train people in various engineering specialties.

The faculties of arts and sciences were not true teaching institutions until the 1870s. Their function was to examine for and grant the *baccalauréat* to students of the lycées and colleges and the *licence* and the *agrégation* needed by those interested in teaching careers in those institutions. The professors also gave lectures, but these were attended more by a general audience than by students. In the humanities, classical learning was an important part of the examinations at all levels, presumably because of its importance for teaching in the high schools.

Eventually, starting in the 1870s, the faculties of sciences and letters became true and increasingly specialized teaching institutions, and in 1896, the name *university* was reintroduced as a designation for several loosely linked faculties (Prost, 1968; Zeldin, 1967). But, as a matter of fact, different faculties were not merged into something like a real corporate entity until 1968.

Organizationally, the distinguishing characteristic of this system was its complete subjection to the central government. As has been pointed out, this had been the original aim of the French reformers, for whom the enemy was not the government but the privileged groups and institutions. The subjection of the entire system of education to the government was considered a progressive step, especially after the Revolution, when the government became, or was supposed to have become, representative of the people. Philosophers and scientists did not object to government control, especially since the new democracy was meritocratic and used its scientists and philosophers in the formulation of educational policies.

The purpose of these policies was to educate on the primary

level a patriotic and literate citizenry, and to provide on the secondary level a good general education that was not very different from the general education given under the old regime. Higher education was reserved for those who wanted to enter certain careers in the civil service (including teaching in the colleges, lycées, and the faculties), or in such fields of public responsibility as law and medicine. The system did not envisage a general category of privileged learned professions. The examinations—which were usually competitive—and the academic titles were meant only to qualify people for public positions in which specialized expertise was needed. Otherwise, it was up to the individual to acquire whatever education and training he needed.

Teaching in the institutions of higher education was supposed to be scholarly and scientific. Many of the teachers were outstanding scholars and scientists who devoted most of their time (teaching duties were light) to research. But there was no assumption that research had to be performed in the institutions of higher education or that students had to participate in research. The government supported research partly through specialized research institutes, like the *Musée d'Histoire naturelle,* and partly through subsidies to individuals, but this was done separately from the support and organization of teaching.

Thus, the French reforms apparently realized the aim of the eighteenth century critics of the universities and professional corporations. They replaced the educational monopoly of the universities and the status privileges of the learned professions by what appeared to be a set of pragmatic arrangements. Professional training was to consist of what was needed for effective practice, and not of what intellectual authorities like the old universities or the professional guilds thought it should be.

The relationship between the ruling class and the professionals also changed drastically. In principle, both groups lost their closed corporate character. Politicians, civil servants, and professionals were supposed to constitute interlinking meritocracies, entry into which was to be based on individual attainments and not on class and inheritance.

In England, there was no revolution, not even a programmatic overall reform of higher education. The old universities were not abolished, nor were the privileged guilds (Armytage, 1955;

Reader, 1966). Instead, the critics of these institutions, who included members of occupations aspiring to professional status as well as scientists and philosophers, obtained corporate rights of their own and established professional training and licensing schemes and new universities to compete with the old ones. Thus, unlike in France, where control over professional training passed almost entirely into the hands of the government, in England the dualism based on cooperation between universities and professional associations, only residually supervised by the government, was maintained. These reforms did not abolish professional privilege, but made it less invidious by dispersing it much more widely than before. No longer did a single kind of learning or a privileged path lead through the ancient universities of Oxford and Cambridge to the learned professions.

Like the other reforms, the English arrangements implied the abolition of classical learning as the common basis of the learned professions. Classical learning remained an important precondition of professional status, but it was no longer a sufficient condition. The qualifying examinations required increasingly specialized knowledge. Furthermore, apprenticeship, which has always been a part of professional training, became a formalized part of the higher education system.

Thus, in spite of the similarity of the English and French groups of scholars, scientists, philosophers, and lower-grade professionals who spearheaded the reforms of the professions and the universities, and in spite of the similarity of their ideas, the systems that emerged in the two countries differed greatly. The privileges of the professional guilds were under attack, and the relevance of traditional learning for the professions was questioned both in France and in England. There was also an agreement that the idea of the "learned professions" had to be replaced by a variety of academic and practical training schemes. But in France the autonomy of professional guilds (including that of the universities) was abolished, and they were replaced by a system of specialized institutions and examinations centrally devised and supervised by a professional civil service. The British government was much more reluctant to assume responsibility for higher (or other) education. Apart from some private hospital medical schools, in England there were only three government institutions and one private institution like the specialized French *écoles des applications:* the Royal Military Academy, Woolwich, which trained artillery and engineering officers; the Government School of Mines and of Science Applied to the Arts (1851) (later Royal School of Mines); and the Normal School of Science (1872). The private school was the Royal College of Chemistry, which was eventually absorbed into the Royal School of Mines. In 1907 the two civilian scientific schools were merged in the Imperial College of Science and Technology and became part of the University of London. Training remained in the hands of universities and professional associations. Organizationally, the only change before the middle of the nineteenth century was that new associations and new universities were added to the old.

In Germany, the movement for the reform of higher education consisted entirely of philosophers and scholars, a group different from those who initiated the reform in France and in England. Occupational groups aspiring to professional status played no role in the movement, because they were weak and because they were dispersed in many small and medium-sized cities. Unlike France and England, Germany consisted of many small independent states, and did not have a center like Paris or London where all the important things happened. This also had an effect on the intellectuals, but less so than on the professional people, because books and journals circulated widely. Therefore, the whole target of the movement was the acquisition of university privileges for the new philosophers and scholars. They did not want privileges to be abolished, but to be shared through the establishment of a new type of university.

The role of the Prussian government was different from that of either the French or English. It was strong and intent on controlling everything, as was the government in France, but the old regime was not entirely abolished in Germany until the end of World War I. Therefore, the reforming scholars and philosophers could not consider themselves part of the ruling elite, nor could they trust the government as their counterparts did in France. But because of its respect for traditional forms, the German government was willing to grant a measure of corporate autonomy to the new universities, since corporate autonomy had been consistent with the legal ideas of the old regime.

Thus, the reformed university emerged as a monopolistic institution for professional education.[1] The importance of the academies and specialized professional schools established in the seventeenth and eighteenth centuries (especially the latter) for the cultivation of the natural sciences and for the teaching of medicine and engineering declined. Medicine was completely reabsorbed into the universities, and engineering, which was not, had to accept a status inferior to the university professions until the very end of the nineteenth century.

Thus, instead of diminishing the importance of the universities, the German reform reinforced their importance, reversing thereby the earlier trend to replace them with professional schools.

This reversal did not mean an abandonment of either of the two goals of higher educational reform. The reformed university was to be modern in its emphasis on philosophy and up-to-date scholarship. It did not assign a great role to the experimental sciences in the curriculum only because their intellectual importance and their potential as disciplines of advanced study were not yet fully recognized. These fields were accorded a place that seemed commensurate with their importance. After all, even in France, where their importance was fully recognized, the natural sciences were not granted much of a place in the Napoleonic educational system.

The invidious aspects of university privileges were also ostensibly eliminated. The university was to be a prestigious and even privileged institution, but this privilege was to be based on true scholarly merit, not on traditional status bolstered by a general, and usually shallow, humanistic learning. Above all, the privileges of the old professional faculties of theology, law, and medicine, which were the most offensive to the philosophical and scholarly intellectuals, were eliminated. The professional faculties were no longer considered the higher faculties for which the arts and sciences faculty served as mere preparation. All faculties now became equal and had the right to confer the same degrees, including the doctoral degree. In fact, the philosophy faculty became the most important. With the elimination of the traditional privileges of the professional

[1] For an authoritative description of the nineteenth-century German university see Paulsen (1902/1966).

groups that had ruled the faculties of law and medicine, scholarly attainments also became the criteria of appointments to the professional faculties.

As has been pointed out, missing from the German reform movement were low-grade professionals demanding equality of privilege with the old learned professions or the abolition of all guildlike professional privilege. But these professionals were significant only in England. In France, equality of professional opportunity was ensured through the government's taking over the entire system of higher education and examinations for the qualifying degrees for professional work. The reformed German university, with its freedom of study and examinations based strictly on merit, served this purpose equally well. In fact the government usually required further qualifying examinations for the license to practice medicine, law, and even teaching. Thus the German reform, as the French one, modernized the curriculum and replaced traditional academic and professional privilege with a system of educational advancement based on merit and, directly or indirectly, controlled by the government.

The lack of differentiation in the German system of higher education, which was based on a single type of university, resulted from the relative lack of articulation in the German society (Brunschwig, 1974, pp. 119–163). The middle classes had little political influence and no effective organization. The Prussian government, and subsequently the governments of the other German states, could therefore maintain, and even strengthen, the privileges of the universities and their professors. Of course, this did not confirm traditional privilege, but promoted new privilege based—in principle—entirely on scholarly merit. But because the administration and the adjudication of this merit were placed into the hands of the academic profession, with only residual powers vested in the state, the "professorial estate" was privileged to an extent that would have been inconceivable at that time in France and that was also against the general trend of abolishment of status privileges in Germany itself.

ASCENDANCY OF THE GERMAN SYSTEM Paradoxically, by the middle of the nineteenth century the relatively undifferentiated German system became far more influential than the other two. Whereas the economic and political life in Germany followed the more industrialized and more democratic France and England, the reverse happened in academic life, especially in England. The pluralism of higher education in mid-century England was reduced largely as a result of attempts to follow the example of the German universities, and by the turn of the century the English system became—very much like the German one—increasingly homogeneous and based on universities.

The trend favoring the university, rather than a system based on a plurality of institutional types, stemmed from the great success of German universities in specialized scientific and scholarly research. Until about the 1870s, German universities were virtually the only institutions in the world in which a student could obtain training in how to do scientific or scholarly research. It was known that this superiority in research was not accompanied by equal superiority in training for professional practice (Billroth, 1924, pp. 41–98) or in the education of those who did not intend to become either scientists or professionals, but excellence in professional practice, or in education for its own sake, was much more difficult to measure than excellence in research. Furthermore, researchers, unlike practicing professionals, competed with each other internationally, and it was extremely frustrating for English or French scientists, working without aid in their makeshift laboratories, to compete with their German counterparts, who worked in well-appointed university laboratories with large numbers of students and assistants (Cardwell, 1957, pp. 46–51, 89–92, 134–137; Guerlac, 1964, pp. 85–88).

The success of German research was attributed to the German university: first to its principle of "unity of research and teaching," but also to its being a general rather than a specialized institution, and to its self-government. As a matter of fact, as will be shown, the success of German research was due mainly to the intensive courses of training originally intended for teachers (seminars) and pharmacists (chemical laboratories) that developed far beyond their original purpose into university research institutes as a result of the intense competition between the universities of the different states. These historical conditions notwithstanding, the fact was that the only system of research and training was the German one.

The reaction to this challenge in the second half of the nineteenth century was very different in England and in France. In England the universities of great prestige and wealth, Oxford and Cambridge, had the means and the wish to maintain their status in the changed intellectual climate of the nineteenth century. They were challenged by the new university colleges in London and elsewhere that catered to the needs of the upcoming professional classes. To compete with those institutions on their own ground of professional training would have been inconsistent with the elite standing of Oxford and Cambridge. Adopting the German model of cultivating research was a way to modernize themselves and yet maintain their elite status in a manner which was legitimate by democratic standards—namely, through scientific excellence—without connecting themselves directly to some actual bread-and-butter purpose.

The result was an actually improved version of the original Humboldtian university ideal (Ashby, 1967, p. 5; Flexner, 1930, pp. 274–278). The old English universities concentrated on teaching and research in the basic arts and sciences; taught law as part of the humanities; and, in medicine, taught only the basic medical sciences, leaving clinical training to hospital medical schools. Thus professional studies were really subordinated to disciplinary ones, while in Germany the professional faculties continued to be separate and numerically very strong in spite of the dominant ideology of disciplinary research. Finally, the autonomy of Oxford and Cambridge, as corporations of scholars, was much greater than that of the German universities. These two British universities had their own wealth and were not dependent on the government for either finances or honors, as the German universities were.

With Oxford and Cambridge adopting the German model, the pioneering university colleges and specialized schools lost much of their glamour. To serve as mere "community service stations" without also representing a new cultural ideal was not inspiring. So they began to imitate Oxford and Cambridge, a trend greatly reinforced by the fact that many of their teachers were trained at those universities. Thus a university-based system arose in England. But this was far from a replica of the German model. As will be seen in the analysis of the different university systems, the English system managed to preserve much of its diversity even after the decline of institutional pluralism. And it has never abandoned entirely such pluralism. In spite of an insistence on like standards, universities have been of different quality, and there have also been differences in program and emphasis among them. Finally, starting from 1913, research councils were established by the government to found nonuniversity research institutes for large-scale organized research that was deemed to be of public interest.[2]

The German challenge was also felt in France, but there, in the absence of viable universities, it had much less impact. A group of reformers emerged in 1880, the *Société de l'enseignement supérieur,* who advocated the creation of universities in the German-English mode, and some efforts were made toward making the university into a seat of research. But this was never carried out consistently. Instead, the government created new institutions; first, in 1868, the *Ecole pratique des hautes études,* which coordinated and supported research in the different schools and university faculties. Eventually (in 1939) this function was taken over by the *Centre national de la recherche scientifique,* while the *Ecole pratique* took its place among other institutions providing employment for research workers and practical training for students interested in research. Even the reform of 1968, the purpose of which was to make the university into a relatively autonomous body and to unify teaching and research, did not change the character of the system. The specialized *grandes écoles* continued to be the core and the top of the system, and, as will be shown below, the system still operates as a centralized whole, divided into separate functional units rather than as a system of competing autonomous universities (Zeldin, 1967).

THE AMERICAN SYSTEM The American system, which emerged in its modern form between the 1860s and the turn of the century, had a history different from the European ones (Veysey, 1965). The old American system shared with the old European systems their almost exclusive emphasis on classical learning and their poor standards of scholarship. But there were neither educational nor

---

[2]There had been nonuniversity research institutes in Germany, too, before there were any in England. But they did not become as important a part of the system. (See Organisation for Economic Co-operation and Development, 1967a, p. 51.)

professional monopolies in the United States, so that no particular group clamored to make the system more just and to base it on merit rather than on status. There was only a general democratic pressure to make higher education accessible to all the strata of society.

The second requirement of modernization, to update the scientific curriculum, was also based on social premises different from those of Europe. In each of the European countries that have been discussed, there were competent scholars and scientists who wanted to replace the ineffective old-type university faculty. Their demand for reform was to some extent also a struggle of new classes of intellectuals to take over the system from the incompetent incumbents.

In the United States few scientists and scholars were competent enough to replace the incumbents, and the reform movement was not a struggle between entrenched privilege and frustrated aspirations. The foremost purpose of the reform was to catch up with European higher education. Dissatisfaction with the existing state of affairs did not arise from internal disputes, but from contact with superior foreign models. In this sense the case of the United States was one of "secondary reform" and belongs to the same category of externally inspired change as the establishment of modern systems of higher education in Russia, Japan and elsewhere in Asia, and Africa.[3]

Thus, the system that emerged was like the German and the English ones—a university system. Since the federal government did not assume responsibility for higher education, it would have been impossible to establish a centrally directed system of specialized institutions, as in France. In those state systems in which central direction and division of functions between institutions was possible, some attempts were made to create differentiated systems of state universities and state colleges, but eventually the latter also developed into universities. Indeed such was the dominance of the German universities that it would have been difficult to imagine any country choosing the French model. Even Japan, a highly centralized country

[3] Lipset (1963, p. 2) made the general point that the patterning of many of the institutions of the United States after European models marked the beginning of a historical process of founding "new nations" through conscious deliberation and planning.

with an interventionist government to which the French system was actually much more congenial than a university system, followed the German model in higher education.

But the American university was and has remained something very different from either the German or the English one. In Europe demand for educational equality was satisfied by the abolition of educational and professional privilege and the establishment of systems of higher education based on merit. In the United States there was a much more powerful demand to actually extend higher educational opportunities to broad strata of the population, not only to those entering the traditional professional occupations. As a result, general higher education, either as a preliminary to advanced studies or as a terminal education, remained part of higher education even after the reform of the curriculum, and so did lower-grade professional studies (which were eliminated from it in England and France after some initial experiments).

The effect of the German system was manifested in the graduate school, which did not replace the college, but was added to it as a seat of higher-level study. The graduate school that trained students for the doctoral degree was an improved version of the German university research institutes, just as the reformed Oxford and Cambridge were improved versions of German undergraduate education.

Thus the American university system, although based on actually or potentially equivalent units (every college could become a university, and many did), was in fact a highly differentiated system. Differentiation in this system was open and recognized, unlike in England, where it was concealed. Even the differences in quality were much more openly admitted and tolerated than in England. But the differentiation of functions (unlike that of quality) took place mainly within institutions, and not between them, as it did in France.

A NEW NOTION OF HIGHER EDUCATION By the beginning of this century, all systems of higher education—with the partial exception of those in Spanish- and Portuguese-speaking countries—were reformed. In the educationally developed European countries, these reforms were a result of internal intellectual and social developments. Elsewhere, such as in the United States, or in newly established systems, such as in Japan (Bartholomew, 1971), the new higher education was modeled on the advanced European, and particularly the German, example.

As has been seen, the systems that emerged in the course of the nineteenth century differed from each other in their organizational structure, their dependence on central government, their curricula, and the emphasis they placed on different aspects of research and teaching. However, in spite of these variations, the idea of what constituted higher education was common to all the systems. It was that education at this level had to be based on specialized science and scholarship and that it had to be linked to research, at least to the extent that professors were expected to be qualified and successful researchers. Furthermore, the idea was that the proper scope of higher education consisted of the basic arts and sciences, of professional studies based on basic sciences like medicine, and of professional studies that, like law and theology, possessed an elaborate intellectual tradition of their own.

This was somewhat different from the ideas of the late-eighteenth- and early-nineteenth-century reformers of higher education who did not connect empirical and especially experimental research with teaching, and who conceived of professional education as a kind of vocational education rather than something closely related to the basic arts and sciences. Still, the achievements of nineteenth-century higher education were consistent with the principles of the reformers of the late eighteenth and early ninteenth centuries, if not with their detailed plans. The new higher education was built on modern science and scholarship and not on classical erudition, and it conferred professional status on the basis of specific competence in given fields, rather than on the basis of examinations testing general educational accomplishment or on membership in privileged guilds.

The specificity and universality of the criteria according to which degrees were conferred satisfied society's sense of social justice and intellectual honesty. In principle all the reformed systems of higher education were perfectly meritocratic and pragmatic. That they were designed only for the education of an elite was not considered invidious as long as the selection of students seemed just; as long as there was no doubt about the need for a well-trained class of doctors, lawyers, high school and university teachers, and higher civil servants; and as long as it was believed that the existing higher educational systems trained their students reasonably well for these tasks.

However, by the beginning of this century there were many signs that the conception of higher education as a combination of research and disciplinary study leading to professional qualification was in need of revision. The emergence of specialized, nonuniversity research institutes beginning in the 1880s, and the retention of the liberal arts degree and the creation of a large variety of professional and semiprofessional degrees in the United States (and after the First World War also in the Soviet Union), suggested that the combination of research with single-level and essentially professional studies that was accepted in Europe might not be the optimal mix of functions. This impression was also confirmed by developments in the European countries themselves, especially by the emergence of specialized, nonuniversity research institutes in all the European countries between the 1880s and the First World War.

Nevertheless, those ideas remained largely unchanged until the Second World War, and the functions and scope of higher education have still not been clearly reconceptualized. This has been partly due to the inertia of the European systems, which, by and large, dominated the academic scene until the Second World War, and partly because higher education has been judged primarily according to its success in research, which is its most prestigeful and most cosmopolitan function. An attempt at rethinking the functions of higher education began only in the 1960s.

The following chapters will trace how the main functions of higher education have evolved in the different systems and how this evolution affects their present-day performance.

3. Education for the Professions

The assumption that advanced education needed to be specialized, and that specialized study was necessary for a professional career, was the basis of the transformation of higher education in the nineteenth century. Even where there was a strong ideology against splitting scholarship into specialities and viewing university studies as a preparation for careers, as in Germany and in the elite English universities, specialization became the rule. However, the relationship between study and career remained much more complicated than had been envisioned by some of the early advocates of educational reform. The study of specialized disciplines in Germany and in the elite English universities came to be regarded in many cases as the way to obtain a "real" liberal education that would qualify the student to be part of the intellectual elite, rather than serve as preparation for professional work. Only by acquiring deep knowledge in a single field and watching at close range a professor exploring the frontiers of knowledge was one thought to have obtained advanced education. Although this was mainly rhetoric for most students, since they learned what they did in order to enter specific careers, a minority of students studied without worrying about a career, and for many others studying for its own sake was at least a meaningful ideal.

Furthermore, some schools that were originally set up for specific training purposes and that continued to be regarded mainly as providing preparation for specific careers actually developed broad-gauged programs. For example, the curriculum of the *Ecole polytechnique* in Paris now includes mathematics, science, and some economics and humanistic studies, constituting a kind of liberal arts program.

Thus, some highly specialized courses of study could be

considered liberal arts programs if classified according to the intentions of some of their students; conversely, by using the same criterion, courses including a wide range of subjects without relating them to the needs of a specific professional practice could be considered a professional program.

The criterion for classifying a program to be adopted in this chapter will be the destination of most of the students in that program. As a study of Ushiogi (1971, p. 367) has shown, about 70 to 80 percent of the graduates of all higher education in the advanced countries of Europe, and of American graduate schools (though not of American colleges or junior colleges), end up in professional or administrative occupations, and, presumably, study for this purpose.

Ushiogi also found that the fraction of university graduates in the total working population in Europe is about the same (4 percent) as the fraction of those possessing second or third degrees in the United States working population. Ushiogi's data are for 1960, when the postwar expansion of higher education was already well on its way. Thus it can be assumed that the fraction of graduates in professional occupations was even higher than 80 percent in earlier years. It is justified, therefore, to speak of higher education in England, France, and Germany as mainly a professional education.

Accordingly, the term *professional education* will be used here loosely to describe all specialized or nonspecialized higher education that is usually acquired with a view to entering specific occupations. According to this definition, all higher education except the American liberal arts course, some of the first degrees in Japan and other Asian countries where there has been a proliferation of colleges of unequal standards, and perhaps some small-scale experiments elsewhere, is professional education. Nonprofessional education will be called *general higher education.*

The word *profession* will be used in a similarly loose sense to denote all the occupations into which entry is generally limited to those possessing diplomas from institutions of higher education. Therefore, higher civil service, or other administrative and managerial services that recruit entrants from university graduates, will be considered professions, although no specific higher education is technically necessary for such careers.

This definition of profession is broader than those that

restrict the term to occupations based on a highly specialized branch of knowledge.[1] One reason for preferring the broader definition is that the usual, narrow definition is difficult to apply. In some cases, such as higher-level administration, people trained specifically for their work are employed in the same capacity as others who did not obtain such training. Problems in classifying such occupations would arise in using the narrow definition. If higher-level administration is not considered a profession because of the absence of a consensus about what constitutes specialized knowledge in that field, then a degree in public or business administration would not be a professional degree either. But what else would it be? The question becomes even more difficult in countries where entrance to the civil service is (or was in the past) limited to people possessing a degree in law. In such instances, specialized knowledge is required, but that knowledge is related primarily to a different occupation. One would then have to say that civil servants in such countries are professionals, but that civil service is not a profession; and that all civil servants have to possess professional degrees, but that there is no professional education for the civil service.

Therefore, a realistic definition has to recognize that the relationship between higher education and what are called professions is much more complex than it is made to appear in the current literature. In fact, in very few professions is practice directly *based* on some kind of theoretical or other specialized disciplinary knowledge. There is rather a scale of relationships between specialized knowledge and practice. Exceptions are teaching and research, chemistry, some fields of engineering, and medicine. But in most kinds of engineering and medicine, though practice may require frequent recourse to specialized knowledge, the use of this knowledge is intuitive and guided by experience. Finally, in such professions as social work there is also recourse to specialized knowledge, but the range of potentially relevant knowledge is so wide that it is impossible to delimit it to a relatively coherent field. To the extent that social workers should be individuals with a proven capacity to

[1] Thus the present definition differs from the census category of "professional and technical workers." But essentially the same conception of "professional" is adopted by Carr-Saunders and Wilson (1933, pp. 239–245, 491–503) and Marshall (1950, pp. 128–155).

acquire and make use of specialized knowledge when the need arises, and that they should have the ability to find and evaluate potentially relevant specialized knowledge, it is justified to require them to have higher educational qualifications. Of course, what the most appropriate qualifications are may be debatable, but this is also not easy to decide in such a profession as engineering (for the most part), or medicine, where recourse is made to a more limited, but still broad range of knowledge.

Another reason for not insisting on a narrow definition of professional education requiring the existence of an *intrinsic relationship* between a field of specialized knowledge and an occupation is that specialized knowledge does not make a profession. Surgeons and engineers in the past, or simultaneous translators and computer programmers in the present, have had highly specialized knowledge but have not been considered professional people at all, or they have had less prestige than, for example, lawyers, whose knowledge is less specialized and more accessible to the general public than that of the engineer, the surgeon, the translator, or the programmer. The privileges of professional status and its requirement of higher education arose not so much from the difficulty and the specificity of the professional function, but from anxiety about the potentially far-reaching consequences of professional work. Professional occupations deal with matters in which an unusual amount of harm or good can be done. Doctors, and occasionally lawyers, deal with matters of life and death. The loss or gain to a firm that can be caused by an engineer exceeds by several orders of magnitude the loss or gain that can be caused by a manual worker. The negligence of the worker can spoil one day's labor, but that of the engineer can spoil 100 or 10,000 days of labor (Stinchcombe, 1963). There are similar considerations concerning the work of senior civil servants, university professors (the teachers of teachers), and managers of large industrial firms.

Employers and other users of the services of such persons are in a difficult situation. They rarely possess the knowledge required to judge the competence of the professional person; and the results of such professional work as law, general medicine, or higher civil service are altogether difficult to evaluate unequivocally. In other types of professional work, such as engineering or scientific research, evaluation by results is easier, but even in these one cannot judge a person reliably until a very long time after his or her employment begins. Therefore, patients and clients try to avoid risks and to obtain some degree of certainty by relying on degrees or similar qualifications that indicate that the person has the intellectual ability, the competence, and the moral character (the possession of high qualification is also a sign of endurance and responsible behavior) needed for the effective and responsible performance of the job. This is why governments have preferred that higher civil servants have some professional training, and why members of occupations dealing with human affairs, such as social work and counseling, are granted professional status, in spite of their relatively nontechnical work. They deal with delicate personal problems in a society that respects individual autonomy and dignity, a circumstance which seems to require higher educational qualification.

CLASSICAL EDUCATION IN THE PROFESSIONS These broad definitions of professional education and professions fit very well the circumstances of the learned professions of the past, when all these professions were based on classical learning. For the present, however, there may be doubts, even after these considerations, about the usefulness of lumping into a single category types of education that range from the highly specialized to the broadly general only because they serve similar occupational purposes. From the point of view of the universities these are quite different programs. This procedure may be justified, however, by the existence of significant educational elements that these diverse types of education share with the past tradition of the learned professions.

This problem can be clarified through an investigation of the transition from eighteenth- to modern nineteenth-century professionalism. Prior to the nineteenth century, the rationale for basing professional privilege almost exclusively on classical learning was twofold. As has been pointed out, the ability to master Greek and Latin and to interpret classical texts was considered (with some justification) the best available test to general intellectual ability. Furthermore, classical learning had been the main repository of scientific knowledge. This belief was undermined during the seventeenth and eighteenth centuries by the rise of modern physics and astronomy. But before the emergence of modern chemistry and biology toward the end of the eighteenth century, classical learning could still hold its own as an important source of knowledge even for physicians. Someone who wanted to ensure that his soul, body, and legal rights were taken care of by the most competent people not unreasonably preferred practitioners who had had a classical education.

This is not to imply that a search for alternatives could not have led to other types of selection and education for the professions. Educational reformers and philosophers imbued with the spirit of new science put forward such alternatives as far back as the sixteenth century. But a long time elapsed before these doubts and criticisms actually led to reform. There were strong vested interests in the maintenance of the status quo. The established learned professions had the advantage of having a single kind of education as the basis for all advanced knowledge. This made it easier to delimit the range of learning, exclude everything that had no classical antecedent, and thereby maintain the unity of the professions as a status group. This inclination to adhere to the old type of learning was, of course, most marked among academic teachers, themselves members of professions, who had a vested interest in maintaining the intellectual supremacy of their disciplines.

But vested interest in the system alone could not have maintained it. The old traditions were difficult to break mainly because the institutions of higher education managed to attract (through their prestige, and by stipends and other benefits) nearly all the young people with the ability and the motivation for higher study. It was therefore difficult to find suitable candidates for professional work outside the ranks of those possessing a classical scholarly education. Thus the argument that such education was a necessary condition of professional competence could be supported by plausible evidence.

Had the universities been able to continue attracting a high proportion of the ablest young men, their insistence on classical education as a basis for professional standing could probably have been prolonged. But concomitant with the growth of science and a new type of scientific philosophy was a decline in the attractiveness, and probably also in the standards, of the universities. Nicholas Hans has shown that the fraction of contributors to science who had studied at universities declined in eighteenth-century England, and that the universities lost their reputation as seats of learning (Hans, 1951, pp. 31–34). Only when the quality of classical learning declined did the criticism leveled against the universities and old-type learning lead to the reforms that began in France in the 1790s.

PROFESSIONAL PRIVILEGE The overt function of classical learning in professional training was to ensure that people performing certain vital functions would be of high intellectual quality. At the same time the requirement of classical education also closed the professions, protected them from free competition, and conferred on them monopolistic privileges. These privileges, which are ubiquitous in the history of the learned professions, are the result of the scarcity of talent required in such work. Because of this scarcity, the powerful and the rich have always tried to monopolize the services of professionals. But these are not easy to monopolize, because professional people have a natural monopoly that they prefer to exploit to their own advantage. Scarce resources of talent and knowledge cannot be taken away from their owners, nor can their owners be coerced to use their talents and knowledge effectively according to the whims of powerful clients. Therefore, professionals have always been in a strong bargaining position, even when their clients were rulers and other powerholders. Merchants could be robbed of their wealth, and peasants could be compelled to work the land, but professional people had to be pleased.

The only way to affect the bargaining power of professionals is to control their training. To some extent, training will always be controlled by the professionals themselves, since only they are capable of training others. But governments can weaken professional privilege by creating or encouraging universities and professional schools that are independent of the practitioners; by withholding the right of licensure from a professional association and granting it to institutions of higher education; and by creating institutions for some specific purpose, such as the training of priests, astrologers, army officers, or government lawyers. In many parts of the world, professional education actually started in such government-sponsored training schools (Grimm, 1960).

Rulers, however, could effectively control the transmission only of specific techniques. They could preempt the esoteric services of clock repairers or gunmakers, but they could not control higher learning, which teaches more than techniques, and which provides scope for intellectual virtuosity and originality. The intellectually ablest have always been attracted to the highest intellectual traditions in society, such as Confucianism, the Talmud, or scholastic and, later, humanistic learning. Such learning became the main criterion of intellectual excellence, so that those who wanted the services of the intellectually most competent had to turn to people possessing this learning. It was almost inevitable that those dealing with matters of justice, health, and salvation should come from among the ranks of the learned. This learnedness also exempted the professions from effective outside control. Rulers could grant or deny charters to universities and could buy their support, but they could not control them as they could control a workshop in which masters trained apprentices. Higher learning remained a monopoly of the learned class.

The decline of classical learning and the rise of specialized sciences and sophisticated technologies seemed to offer an opportunity to break this monopoly. Part of the Baconian utopia was the idea that the new learning would give rise to an intellectual tradition that would spread competence much more widely and much more effectively (Purver, 1967, pp. 24–36). The Enlightenment program to replace the universities with specialized vocational schools directed by an enlightened government was an attempt to realize the Baconian utopia as well as to break the invidious monopolies of the learned professions and the privileged universities. The later liberal attempt to do away with all official higher education and licensing and to throw professional practice open to competition on a free market was an even more radical attempt to eliminate professional privilege.

Indeed, an observer of the professional scene around 1800—before the influence of the German philosophers on university reform was felt—might easily have come to the conclusion that the whole tradition of learned professions was about to come to an end, alongside all other guildlike organizations. A physician or a lawyer obviously needed specialized knowledge, but a conviction grew that it was nobody's business to ask where and how that knowledge was acquired, or whether, in addition to the technically necessary knowledge, the person also possessed classical or any other kind of education.

However, as the description of the reform of the system of higher education in the three European countries has shown, the plans to abolish professional privilege did not work. Although general opinion held that the professions were not different from other occupations and that special arrangements for professional education and licensure should be abolished, institutions were erected, and new procedures for education and licensing merely replaced the old. Apart from a very short period during the French Revolution (1793–1794), complete laissez faire has never been the rule in professional training. As has been seen, the shape and character of the new institutions reflected the views of the upcoming groups of professionals and the intellectuals. Governments, which were supposed to represent the public interest, merely acted as arbiters between the new professionals and intellectuals and those who defended the old universities and the old professional corporations. The governments modified the views finally adopted, but did not actually initiate policy. France—where higher education was planned and regulated by the government according to specific social needs—was an exception. But the exception was more apparent than real, since, as has been pointed out, the post-Revolutionary ruling group included many of the reformist scientists and philosophers. Even an autocratic ruler like Napoleon, who made drastic changes in primary and secondary education, did not interfere much with professional education.

The wish of governments to break the monopolies of professional guilds manifested itself, not in the adoption of a laissez faire attitude or in autocratic control, but in a preference for entrusting professional education to academic institutions rather than to apprenticeship and courses organized by the professional associations. This preference was particularly conspicuous in Germany, where the universities obtained an actual monopoly of professional education. But it was also the case in France, where control of the system was vested in what might be described as a kind of mandarinate, the members of which both taught in the new institutions of higher education and administered the whole system of education from the ministry of education. Initially this trend was not conspicuous in

England, but it appeared there, too, about the middle of the nineteenth century. This, of course, could be and was interpreted as a step toward weakening professional privilege. The new institutions of higher education considered themselves representatives of the broadest interests of the public, and their members were convinced of the social utility of higher learning. Scientific study was considered a means of ensuring high-quality professional services because it regulated the entry into professions according to intellectual merit and provided future professionals with the optimal intellectual background for the performance of their functions.

There is no reason to doubt the sincerity of those who advanced this purpose for desiring to raise the quality of the professions. But they did not entirely abolish professional privilege. After more or less prolonged conflict, some kind of professional privilege based on certification by officially recognized institutions of higher education was reestablished everywhere. And the United States, which had had no professional privileges in the past, established them early in this century. This suggests that an underlying continuity persisted throughout the reforms of higher education in the different countries, that is, the conferral of privilege through higher education of a kind that has been more than the acquisition of sophisticated vocational techniques. This kind of education has included contact with a source of publicly recognized truth, the mastery of which has been considered a test of superior intellectual ability—namely, classical learning in the past, and scientific knowledge based on research in the present. This continuity justifies treating professional education as a single category and investigating the mechanisms that recreated professional privilege in the different countries.

PROFESSIONAL STUDIES IN FRANCE The rationale of the French system has been the most straightforward. It was designed to provide professionals needed for public services, such as the different branches of the military forces, the general and technical civil service, teaching, law, medicine, and pharmacy; to facilitate the acquisition of professional training; and to prevent professional corporations from monopolizing the provision of such training (although, in the case of medicine and law, this was not carried out consistently). The first of these, namely, the need of the military and civil services for highly trained manpower of different kinds, can be determined with some accuracy. Therefore, admission to the institutions designed for the training of this manpower, namely, the principal *grandes écoles* and *écoles des applications,* has been limited, and the training given in them has been intensive and adapted specifically to the particular purpose of each school. On the other hand, it is difficult to determine the need for professional manpower of "society in general." Accordingly, other parts of the higher educational system are much less selective and the training in them much less structured. Admission to the universities, previously faculties, has always been much easier than to the *grandes écoles,* and outside the medical faculty the course of study has been relatively unstructured. Only examinations for the conferral of academic degrees are serious, although they were considerably relaxed after 1968. In addition there have been institutions offering training in various fields, such as the *Conservatoire national des arts et métiers;* a variety of engineering schools like the *Institut national des sciences appliquées* (INSA); the *Institut universitaire de technologie* (IUT); and the *Ecole pratique des hautes études,* to which admission has been even more liberal and flexible.

The division has not been watertight, since the functions of the two types of institutions have overlapped at every stage. Many of those studying at the universities go into government service, and quite a few of the graduates of the *Polytechnique* and of the *écoles des applications* end up in the private sector. About one-third of the students who go to the *grandes écoles* take a university degree as well (some of them, those studying at the *Ecole normale supérieure,* have to take a degree), and graduates of the university sit for the competitive examinations for the *agrégation* alongside students of the *Ecole normale supérieure,* which specifically prepares for it. Furthermore, the *agrégation* is conferred by the universities (Burn, 1971, pp. 7–35). But, apart from the *Ecole normale supérieure,* which is integrated into the university system and constitutes its pinnacle, there is still a distinct difference between the destinations of those who go to the *grandes écoles* and those who go to the universities. The latter go into teaching and higher education, while the former end up mainly in government service and industry (Organisation for Economic Co-operation and Development, 1966, p. 67).

This dual system ensures that those who go to the closed-entry *grandes écoles* are an elite, a small proportion of those who take the classical and literary *baccalauréat*, and a much larger one of those who take the mathematical-technological ones. Admission to the *grandes écoles* requires passing the *baccalauréat* examination and then studying in special preparatory classes for the difficult entrance examinations to the *grandes écoles* themselves. While attending the schools, students are further coached for other examinations geared to the requirements of the technical civil service, or of high-level teaching. Those who want to become practicing engineers often go on to one of the *écoles des applications*, where they obtain intensive training.

In contrast, the university system requires only a *baccalauréat* as a qualification for entrance, and in some cases (for example, the IUT) even less. Most of the time, teaching at the universities has been ineffective. Actually, the university is, or at least was as recently as 1968, more an examining and degree-granting, than an educational and training, institution. What the *grandes écoles* have done intensively and effectively for a small elite of the students, selected to fill definite slots in the economy, the universities have done superficially and ineffectively for the nonelite, who are expected to find their own place after graduation. While the dropout rates at the *grandes écoles* are minimal, those at the universities are high, probably about 60 percent (Poignant, 1969, pp. 196–197).

This gap between an elite higher education in the *grandes écoles* and a nonelite one at the universities was not planned. All higher education was highly selective (except the *Conservatoire*), because the *baccalauréat*, which was a condition of admission to the faculties, was a difficult examination. However, because the *grandes écoles* were even more selective than the faculties, and because the careers of their graduates were ensured, they attracted the best students. But even as late as 1900, 90 percent of the teachers employed in public secondary education were *agrégés*. Their possession of this high academic degree is an indication that the instructors and, presumably, the instruction were of a high level.

However, the number of *baccalauréats* awarded annually gradually grew, from 5,717 in 1900 to 32,363 in 1950. Then began a veritable explosion: 77,000 *baccalauréats* were awarded in 1964 and 169,300 in 1967–68 (Burn, 1971, p. 19). Those who obtained this title, which admitted them to the university, grew from 5 percent of the relevant age group in 1900 to 15 percent in 1967 (Burn, 1971, p. 18). This led to a great expansion of the universities that was not accompanied by a similar expansion of the *grandes écoles*. As a result, the gap between the quality of education in the two types of institutions widened (Burn, 1971, p. 19).

The best example of this discrepancy is engineering education. Originally all high-level engineering training was given at the *grandes écoles*. In the course of the nineteenth century new schools of engineering were established mainly to train engineers for private industry in fields that were not sufficiently cultivated by the existing *grandes écoles*. But engineering education was still given in specialized schools. Today, in addition to the specialized schools, the number of which expanded to cover such specialties as telecommunication and electricity, the majority of engineers are educated at universities and other newly founded engineering schools of lower prestige. Thus the *Ecole polytechnique* and the *écoles des applications*, which constituted in the beginning the entire system of higher engineering education, have become the elite schools in a system of which they form only about one-third (Organisation for Economic Cooperation and Development, 1966, p. 61).

There may be questions about the kind of education given to the elite. It is possible to justify a larger investment in the education of the most able students, who, presumably, benefit most from education, than in the education of the less able. But do they receive the best intensive education? In the most important schools, like the *Polytechnique*, the *Ecole normale*, the *Ecole nationale d'administration*, and the *Ecole libre des sciences politiques*, students receive an education that is, to a large extent, cramming. They are taught by good crammers who prepare them well to pass examinations. Those who go on to the *écoles des applications* receive a thorough, practically oriented training.

This means that, unlike the other systems, the French one deemphasizes research and independent study in elite higher education. It provides the best students with an education that, in the United States, for example, is given to the second best. The *agrégation* and the examinations given at the *Polytechnique* or the *Ecole nationale d'administration* require an erudition that is envisaged in the United States and Canada in the new higher degrees, such as the Doctor of Arts and M.Lit., namely, breadth of knowledge and ease of exposition. The courses at the *écoles des applications* provide a training that can be compared to a strong professional master's program in the United States.

One can also compare the advanced French examinations in content and intent with the civil service examination or with the qualifying examinations of different professional bodies, such as the Royal College of Physicians in England. Some candidates for the English examination also prepare in cramming schools, but those are private schools that prepare students only for examinations, and no particular prestige is attached to them. The high-prestige educational institutions in England have been the leading universities.

Giving elite students intensive coaching for examinations is contrary to the widespread view that the most able students are self-directed and that they can benefit most from free, nondirected study and from contact with intellectually creative teachers. Of course, acceptance at a *grande école* also allows free study, since, as mentioned previously, many of the students attend courses at the university. But they are not always encouraged to acquire a thorough knowledge in some discipline and to participate in research. In this respect the *Ecole normale* differs from the other institutions, and policy within some of the other institutions has changed recently. In any case, it is impossible to decide on the basis of available evidence that making cramming compulsory, and free study and research optional for the best students, is worse preparation for teaching, civil service, and technology than the other way around. It is probably not the best preparation for research, and it is likely that the French system channels a higher proportion of the best talents in mathematics and the natural sciences into practical fields and a lower proportion into research than in the other countries here discussed, but whether this is an advantage or disadvantage is not a question of principle but of supply and demand for researchers and other professionals.

It is more difficult to justify the elevation of cramming schools into elite institutions. Any system of cramming and competitive examinations selects two types of students: those who are able, and those who can cram. By focusing the work of elite institutions on preparation for competitive examinations, a considerable proportion of good learners who have neither much competence nor outstanding talent are likely to pass into the professional elite.

The main problem, however, is the effect that this selection has on the education provided at the universities. While some of the best minds of the country spend years preparing for examinations under the guidance of competent crammers, the less-able students are left to find their own way in the laissez faire atmosphere of the universities. This is like teaching the best swimmers how to swim, and throwing the rest into the river and telling them to reach the shore however they can. It is reasonable to assume that many students who fail, or who pass their examinations without having acquired real competence, could acquire it under a more intensive system of education (Organisation for Economic Co-operation and Development, 1966, p. 57).

This is not to say that the French system provides the opportunity to acquire competence only to those admitted to specialized schools. On the periphery of the university system is an immense variety of opportunities to acquire good training. Those who want to study a discipline in depth and/or to become researchers have access to courses at the *Collège de France* and at the *Ecole pratique des hautes études,* or can apprentice themselves to a research team financed by the *Centre national de la recherche scientifique.* Access to these opportunities is not usually difficult. There are even institutions, such as the *Conservatoire national des arts et métiers* and the less-prestigious engineering schools, to which access is even easier but which still bestow professional or semiprofessional diplomas. However, these are peripheral opportunities. The system provides the framework for intensive training, but the student is left to take advantage of it. Apart from the doctoral degree, and special diplomas that can be obtained here and there, the degree conferred by the university does not bear any evidence that the student took advantage of the opportunity to acquire a more intensive training.

A good example of such a lack of discrimination in the meaning of degrees occurs in medical education (at least prior to 1968) (Jamous & Peloille, 1970). Every medical student is expected to go through a standard course of training that, in its outlines, is similar to those in other countries. But the education received by the majority of students is rather superficial, so that the possession of a degree cannot be regarded as a sufficient guarantee of competence. However, a minority of the students who succeed in obtaining through a competitive examination an *internat* (an apprenticeship at one of the teaching hospitals starting from the fifth year at school) receive an extremely thorough clinical training that is considered outstanding by international standards. While this training makes a great difference in a physician's competence, its presence is not attested by any title (although it is usually advertised on the nameplate of the doctor).

Conversely, passing another competitive examination, the *agrégation*, does not attest either clinical or basic scientific competence. Yet this used to be (and to some extent still is) an important qualification for appointment to teaching positions at medical faculties. In the past, it was actually a more important qualification than success in research. For students interested in medical research, the university faculties of medicine provide poor opportunities. But excellent, though limited, opportunities have been available at the periphery of the system, such as at the *Institut Pasteur*.

The relatively open university structure, of which medical education is an example, has had unintended consequences on educational content. The idea that professional education has to be freely acquired and that universities should provide only the opportunity to study and to take examinations has not worked as expected. Examinations, particularly in a mass system, may not be sufficient evidence of competence and may become not much more than tests of superficial knowledge and the ability to express oneself. Nevertheless, formal grades, which are a prerequisite for professional work, are based on the examinations. As a result the system tends to produce a literary erudition about one's field. Although one acquires specialized knowledge, this knowledge is in fact similar to the classical learning that was considered a precondition to professional status in the pre-Revolutionary era: It is much too often a literary knowledge about a field rather than true mastery of it.

This, by the way, explains one of the apparently strange effects of French higher education, namely, that in spite of its specialized character it produces a relatively large number of general philosophical-literary intellectuals, since good rhetorical and literary skills are the main prerequisites of taking examinations.

We can now compare the original aims of the French system with its actual results. As pointed out, the original purpose was to train experts for the civil service and the professions, and to examine specialized competence and confer degrees accordingly. In fact, much of the system, both at the universities and, perhaps, at the *grandes écoles,* is engaged in imparting verbal-literary skills, a mark of educational status rather than technical competence.

The other original purpose of the system—to abolish professional privilege—was also not fully successful. Indeed, no professional association can effectively control entry into the profession through a monopoly of training and licensing. There is no professional class in France as there is in England and the United States and to some extent even in Germany. But the system produces privilege through education. The dual system, which separates the elite (destined usually for public employment) from the other professionals, and the laissez faire that prevails in the nonelite part of the system have divided the professionally trained into several strata. The elite institutions produce a mandarin class of highly educated people whose success in passing examinations is taken as a sign of general intellectual excellence and establishes a claim to elite positions in government and business. Thus, the symbiotic relationship between a government intent on monopolizing the services of the most talented and best-trained professionals, and a professional class using institutions of professional education to gain monopolistic privileges of status and employment, have been reincarnated by the revolutionary institutions designed to abolish the similar privileges of the old university and university-trained professionals.

The graduates of the more democratic universities differ only in quality, but not in kind, from those of the elite *grandes écoles.* University degrees also test verbal and literary skills rather than specialized competence, but do not place their possessors into privileged positions. Thus university students and graduates are a kind of intellectual lower estate compared to the higher estate of the graduates of *grandes écoles*. While the latter obtain privileges based on general intellectual and cultural qualities, the former claim privileges on the same basis.

Apart from the intellectuals and the mandarins, though partially overlapping with them, are the technically competent professionals whom the system was originally designed to produce. These do not principally identify themselves by their professional qualifications, but by their employment. If they are in private practice, they tend to consider themselves part of the *bourgeois entrepreneur* class, and if they are salaried they consider themselves officials of a certain rank, rather than chemists or engineers. In addition, they may, but do not necessarily, participate in the literary culture of the mandarins and intellectuals. In industry more than half of the senior technical staff still possess less than degree-level diplomas or are trained on the job (Organisation for Economic Co-operation and Development, 1966, p. 67).

Thus the present system is not so different from the system it replaced. French professional education still contains a large element of literary culture, and it still produces both a privileged and a relatively underprivileged educated class. Its goal, to create professional experts who do not consider education a source of privilege, and whose status is a function of their specific individual achievements, has not been realized. Examinations, degrees, and diplomas, though they do not reflect specialized professional competence, nonetheless provide the only access to professional careers. But the revolutionary reforms did abolish the particularistic privileges of university faculties and professional guilds and replaced them with a competitively and honestly selected, and therefore less invidious, meritocracy.

PROFESSIONAL STUDIES IN GERMANY

The problem facing the German reformers was in a way the exact opposite of that which faced their French counterparts. The latter, acting in sympathy with underprivileged professional groups, sought to abolish the monopoly of the universities in professional training and to obtain recognition for new kinds of training adapted to the technical contents of the different professions. The institutions of higher education established in revolutionary France were designed to serve this plurality of training needs. In contrast the German reformers, who wanted to reassert the monopolistic position of the university in higher education, had to show why education for the professions (or at least for the "higher" ones) should remain within the university. They therefore had an interest in finding a common basis for all kinds of professional education.

This was not an easy task, because the old common basis of classical learning had been discredited and because by the end of the eighteenth century it was generally accepted that professional education had to be technically specific and relevant to practice. The difficulty was resolved by making a distinction between the general scientific-philosophical and the more specifically technical elements in professional education. The former was the proper function of the university. The latter could be acquired elsewhere, preferably by apprenticeship. The original idea of the philosophers who propagated the reforms, and in an attenuated form also of Wilhelm von Humboldt, the main designer of the University of Berlin (from which the reform spread to the other universities), was that there was a common philosophical-mathematical and philological basis to all learning and that the study of this basis could serve as the core of all university studies (Schnabel, 1959, p. 456). But in practice this idea did not work. Philosophy lost its attraction, the various disciplines grew further apart, and the university became dominated by the specialized research disciplines of the humanities and of experimental natural science.

However, this specialization still retained a unifying element, namely, research. All disciplinary education at the universities included research. This preserved the common philosophical aim of all university study.

This view of higher education implied a conception of professional education. Learned professions were those occupations with a clear disciplinary basis. The task of the university was to teach this basis adequately, which meant that teaching was to be integrated with research. This was necessary because science and scholarship were an advancing body of knowledge, and only those engaging in research could hope to keep abreast with new developments and be considered fully competent.

However, it was easier to announce the principle than to realize it. Only teaching and research have a clear disciplinary basis of practice, since only teachers and researchers make direct and continuous use in their work of what they have learned at the university. Otherwise the demarcation of a practical professional field never coincides with that of a scientific or scholarly discipline. As long as medicine and law were the only practical fields taught at the university, this discrepancy could be overlooked. Human anatomy, physiology, and pathology had been tied to medicine for many centuries and became identified as medical sciences. And legal studies had been an integral part of the universities for such a long time that it was overlooked that only in part could these studies be considered scholarly. But as a matter of fact, even as early as 1810, when the University of Berlin started operating, there was no intrinsic reason why medicine and law should, while engineering should not, be taught at a university. The absurdity of excluding engineering from the universities became increasingly blatant when, because of the rise of microbiology and biochemistry during the second half of the nineteenth century and early in this century, the variety of "basic" medical disciplines increased. Nevertheless, the universities resisted the incorporation of engineering into the universities, and engineers obtained the coveted status of academic professionals *(Akademiker)* only because the government conferred university status on the technological institutes in 1899.

The case of engineering is only the most notorious one. German universities have been so wary of extending professional training that schools of agriculture, commerce, social work, and the like did not become parts of universities until the 1960s. In fact, the principle that universities had to concentrate on disciplinary teaching restricted even disciplinary innovations. Whenever the question of establishing a new chair in a new field arose, questions were raised about whether it was "really" a new discipline or only a subdiscipline, a "specialty" within an old one, or whether the logical and methodological standards of the field were "really" science or scholarship. The principle that all "true" science, but nothing else, belonged to the universities was too general and abstract to serve as a practical guide for decisions about the academic recognition of innovations. The universities used the principle almost invariably to resist innovations. Nevertheless, the German system was quite innovative in its introduction of new disciplines throughout most of the nineteenth century because the conditions of the academic market encouraged innovation irrespective of the views of academics (Ben-David & Zloczower, 1962).

If we disregard the rationalizations about why certain types of professional and disciplinary education were included in the university curriculum while other types were excluded and try to see what the German universities actually engaged in, it appears that they have been devised for the training of professional teacher-researchers. The disciplinary studies as conducted at the university were directly relevant to this profession. The university also provided supervised apprenticeship for persons preparing for such careers. Seminars, laboratory instruction, and preparation of theses for the doctorate and the *Habilitation* (the most advanced degree, which conferred the right to lecture at a university) provided opportunities and incentives for supervised research apprenticeship, although apprenticeship arrangements were never formalized because research was thought to be a charismatic activity pursued by the creative person on his own. In the training of researchers and teachers, the German system, throughout the nineteenth century, was far superior to all the others. By the 1840s, German universities had become the world's training center for researchers, taking over the lead from Paris.

In the training for other professions, including the training of teachers who did not have an inclination for research, the performance of the system was much less satisfactory. Its advantage, compared to the other systems of higher education throughout most of the nineteenth century, was that the integration of university instruction with research provided a far superior university teacher than the other systems. Furthermore, the principle that universities had to teach only what was scientifically significant provided an excellent criterion for the selection of subject matter (Flexner, 1912, pp. 169–172), and the criterion could be applied because the system was decentralized and competitive. Universities competed for the best researchers, and students had far-reaching freedom in the choice of their courses and even of universities (a student could transfer from one university to the other, carrying with him all his credits, without going through any admission procedures). As a result, meaningless study of boring second-hand material had been largely eliminated from teaching. The teaching was usually of high intellectual quality and quite often brilliant. Students with a minimal degree of good judgment and ability could acquire a very good general education in the disciplines relevant for their future professions.

But an introduction was all that the system routinely supplied. Whether a student would be able to acquire competence in those disciplines was largely up to him. Those who did not want to acquire such competence, or who did not know how to acquire it, could emerge from the system with superficial knowledge. The strict separation of disciplinary studies from the practical training that came afterward in a variety of apprenticeship settings unsupervised by the university could actually serve as a disincentive for serious study. For example, many German students preparing for careers as lawyers or civil servants were, and still are, unable to see the importance of jurisprudence and historical studies of law for their future careers (Rueschemeyer, 1973, pp. 102–103, and 222, fn. 85). Even in medicine, for which clinical training had been organized within the universities,there was a disjunction between this training and the scientific study of the basic fields (Flexner, 1912, pp. 172–173). And little personal attention was given to individual students unless they were to become researchers.

As a result, it was somewhat fortuitous if a student acquired the good disciplinary training that the German universities were believed to offer—even when their reputation was at its peak. In such a field as chemistry, in which disciplinary training and training for practice completely overlapped and in which instruction was based overwhelmingly on laboratory work, German training was probably very good. But in other fields, the scientific education given at the university was regarded by a great many students as a prerequisite for high status rather than as a useful instrument in their future practice. Teachers who were aware of these attitudes usually made no more than token efforts to counteract them by trying to make sure that the students really mastered the subjects they were supposed to. The philosophy that the university was charged only with teaching the "basic" disciplines, but not with practical training, provided an easy justification for slackness in the enforcement of standards. Since the degree of mastery necessary for practice was difficult to determine, it was difficult to establish and enforce generally accepted standards. Consequently, the study of the scientific bases of the professions reverted to something very similar to what the study of the classics had been prior to the nineteenth century. It was a sign of erudition and intellectual quality rather than an instrumentally important part of professional competence. This being the case, there was no serious opposition to the corruption of standards.

Thus, apart from the training of teacher-researchers, the German system of professional training was uneven. Nothing in the German system ensured a reasonable degree of competence. Such competence could be acquired, of course, but a professional degree could also be obtained without competence in either the disciplinary basis, or in the practical art of the profession. What a German degree stood for was very often a quasi-specialized, but actually rather general, philosophical erudition about one's field of studies similar to the results of French education. German university education has also maintained an important element of "general" education in its apparently specialized curriculum. The character of this general education is different from the parallel element in France—it is philosophical rather than literary—but it raises the same problems; namely, it is largely irrelevant for professional competence and its intrinsic intellectual value is likely to be poor, because it is acquired as a by-product of superficial disciplinary study.[2]

Having been designed mainly for the training of teacher-researchers, the system grants principal honor to the researchers. The selection and the education of the elite researcher destined to become a member of the academic profession has been the most highly valued function of the system. Thus, in spite of the absence of a dual system of higher education (as there was in France), the German system has actually worked as a dual system, since it has concentrated a disproportionate effort on the training of an elite and provided a more general education to the bulk of the professionals. But the elite in the German system were the academic researchers, while in France they were dispersed among the leadership positions of the country, primarily in the civil service and higher education. The German system was obviously more effective from the

[2] The survival of the traditional conception of professional hierarchy is attested to also by the continued importance of Latin in both countries until this century (cf. Paulsen, 1921, pp. 569–571; Zeldin, 1967).

point of view of education in general. Because the best researcher-teachers were the elite, the likelihood of a wide diffusion of specialized competence was greater than if civil servants had been the elite. Thus even though education at the university was often superficial and ineffective, there were many good teachers in the high schools, as well as in the specialized institutes of technology, commerce, and the like that were eventually conferred university status. Many competent researchers also entered the chemical and pharmaceutical industries and the hospital system. These specialized institutes, rather than the universities, led to the wide diffusion of competence, especially in technological fields.

The German system has not produced a unified "professional class" like that of England's, but rather a discontinuous hierarchy of intellectual statuses as in France. Professors, as a kind of superprofession, have the highest status and attract the best students. Below them are the university-trained professionals, the *Akademiker,* such as doctors and lawyers, and lower still are the experts who have no full academic standing (such as engineers in the nineteenth century).

The discontinuous hierarchical structure of the highly educated groups and the superficial education of the universities have tended to produce people unable to complete their education or simply uninterested in doing so, preferring the life of the student to that of the professional. This free-floating group is in many ways similar to the French intellectuals. But there is in Germany no mandarin class with a common background of literary erudition and a tradition of participation in politics to counterbalance the antinomian tendencies that arise in these lower intellectual groups.

PROFESSIONAL STUDIES IN BRITAIN

The British system, unlike the French or the German ones, did not have a clearly formulated rationale. The government did not have much of a higher educational policy at any time. It left higher education to the universities and to professional associations and interfered only when it was called upon to arbitrate in specific questions (such as reforms at Oxford and Cambridge), to legislate about licensure, or to grant charters to new colleges and universities and to professional associations. As a result, the conflict between the established associations of the learned professions and the universities of Oxford and Cambridge on the one hand, and the new, less-prestigious professional societies of the apothecaries and solicitors, as well as the new university colleges in London and in the provincial cities on the other hand, was not decided by legislation reforming the whole system, but by a series of decisions about specific issues that, prior to the 1960s, had never added up to an overall policy.

The principal changes in professional education brought about by this piecemeal process were as follows: In the first stage, which ended about the middle of the nineteenth century, increasingly strict schemes of supervised training and examinations were introduced in medicine and law. These schemes were initiated by the lower levels of these professions, usually the apothecaries and the solicitors. By insisting on pragmatic training and on tests of scientific and professional competence, they tried to undermine the elevated standing of the old guilds, whose prestige was based on the family backgrounds of their members and on the classical ("liberal") education they acquired at expensive and exclusive "public" (which elsewhere would be called "private") schools and at Oxford and Cambridge. It was a class conflict in which the groups aspiring to improve their status appealed to universalistic criteria of intellectual, and specific criteria of professional, qualification, as opposed to privileges based on inherited status and vague qualities acquired through "good breeding." The old learned professions fought back and improved their educational standards, but insisted that competence was not enough, that professional practice also required character and breeding. This challenge compelled the new associations to search for further moral and educational credentials. The moral standing of the group could be enhanced by activities designed to increase and diffuse professional knowledge (lectures, publications, and the like), by adherence to a code of ethics, and by obtaining a royal charter. Educational standing could be improved by raising the standards of qualifying examinations and through associations with universities. From this competition between the old and new associations emerged a concept of professionalism that combined the acquisition of specific knowledge and technical competence with membership in professional associations charged with upholding a reasonable level of cultural standards and ethical norms. These standards were enforced through the quality of the examination or, preferably, through education at a university (Carr-Saunders & Wilson, 1933; Reader, 1966).

The transformation of the universities was closely tied to this concept of professionalism. Such universities as Dublin, the Scottish universities, and the London University colleges could successfully compete with Oxford and Cambridge for the new professional clients by offering them specialized courses in science and medicine while also conferring on them the respectability of a university education. Their success eventually compelled the two ancient universities to follow suit and establish their own specialized courses.

This did not grant a monopoly in professional training to the universities. Apprenticeship training and examinations conducted by professional bodies could lead to professional titles in law without study at a university; in engineering, the universities had great difficulty competing with established apprenticeship training; and in medicine, clinical training was given in teaching hospitals that belonged only in name to the universities (Cardwell, 1957, pp. 65–66; Sanderson, 1972, pp. 13–14).

Of course, apprenticeship and specialized training also existed in France, Germany, and in other countries. But only in England was it incorporated into formal programs of training for a professional degree, and only in England were university studies designed to be an integral part of comprehensive training schemes in medicine and law, the two most prestigious professions. In Germany such practical training followed the acquisition of the university degree. In French medical education some attempt was made to integrate practical training into the degree program, but for the large majority of students this was a superficial practical experience, not a systematic apprenticeship.

The second stage in the development of professional education in England started with the introduction of specialized courses of study at Oxford and Cambridge in the 1850s. These specialized courses soon eliminated the necessity of classical, "liberal," education for professional qualification and opened the way to the eventual absorption of the entire training scheme for some professions into the university. This occurred very soon in teaching and research. A teacher of chemistry, or a researcher, could be fully trained in the university by the end of the nineteenth century. Today, this is also true of medicine, engineering, commerce, and several other fields. Thus, what had started out as a gradual integration of university studies into training schemes devised by professional associations ended with the eventual transfer of all the training to the universities. This did not imply abandonment of practical training. Rather, the universities took it upon themselves to organize such training within the universities or under their supervision.

This suggests that, although the system did not have an explicit rationale, it had an underlying one. During the first half of the century, it worked as an imperfect market with many monopolistic elements. Professional associations and universities competed with each other for benefits that could be derived from the organization and development of scarce professional talent. They tried to outdo each other in the improvement and diversification of professional education in order to maintain or to obtain the monopolistic privileges of officially recognized professional status.

What constituted an improvement in the quality of education was not based on a general conception but on ad hoc judgments. The requirements of the Society of Apothecaries were compared with those of the Royal College of Physicians; or the teaching of physiology at University College, London, was compared with what was taught about the subject at Oxford or Cambridge. These comparisons did not raise the basic question of what was a profession or professional education in general. Once the questions of who should be included in the old professions of medicine and law were settled, new ones arose about the professional standing and education of civil servants, teachers, engineers, and the like. The conception of profession was too vague to serve as a guide in these matters. There were no clear-cut criteria to decide what combination of moral responsibility, educational requirement, and technical sophistication justified granting professional monopolies to some vocational organizations and withholding them from others. There was also no clear-cut authority to decide whether an occupation was ripe for professional status. Ultimate authority to close a profession to all but the formally qualified rested with the government. But a profession that had a strong association and that could institute training and qualifying examinations of a reasonably high level was well along the way toward attaining a monopoly even without governmental sanction (Reader, 1966, pp. 71–72). Scottish universities and the new university colleges of London and later also of the provinces played an important role in this development.

But in the middle of the last century, there were still doubts about the value of the universities and their standing. The possibility still existed that specialized institutions would replace them, and some strong professional groups, such as those of the engineers, did not seek university affiliation. Thus, professional privilege had a variety of bases, and there was no consensus about the criteria of professional qualification.

This situation of uncertainty about professionalism changed when the leading and subsequently all other universities adopted the German idea of unity of research and teaching. This unity clearly distinguished university study from other kinds of training for the professions.

If the universities were the only place in which scientific and scholarly education on an advanced level could be acquired, then students for the professions requiring such education had to be trained at universities. And if advanced education meant one based on research, then there was a new common element, replacing classical education, to lend meaning to the notion of "learned" professions. This tilted the balance in favor of the universities as the appropriate seats of professional education and led by slow stages to the domination of professional education by the universities. However, the full effect of charging the universities with exclusive responsibility for professional education was felt in this century only in the United States, which grafted certain features of German university education onto a basically Anglo-Scottish tradition. Before turning now to those developments, I shall attempt to summarize and compare the three cases so far analyzed.

COMPARISON OF THE EUROPEAN SYSTEMS The systems of France, Germany, and Britain had developed their structure during the nineteenth century and preserved it in its essential outlines until the 1960s. They all developed characteristic ways of conferring special privileges on professional groups, of giving preferred treatment to governmental clients, and of organizing professional studies.

The French and the German systems both emphasize the distinction between an elite group and the rank and file of students and destine them for different careers. In France, the elite is educated in *grandes écoles* and receives an education that stresses general intellectual brilliance, erudition, and verbal talent. It is divided into a technocratic and a more literary elite and fills leadership positions in the civil service, higher education, and, to some extent, in big business.[3] In Germany the elite is educated in the universities alongside the rest, but its students receive a more intensive education and are destined for academic careers.

The British system is also based on universities, but it has a hierarchy of universities, with Oxford and Cambridge on the top. The elite students do not receive a markedly more intensive education than do the other students, nor are they channeled into particular positions as are elite students in the other two systems. The British system produces a broad, and in comparison with the other two systems, diversified professional class, the elite of which is as diversified as the whole professional class. Education contributes to the formation of this elite by channeling the best students to the most prestigious universities.

The condition that has made possible the rise of a diversified professional class (including civil servants, academics, and members of the learned professions) in England, in contrast to the stratified educated classes of France and Germany, is the maintenance of professional privilege. This privilege is most conspicuous in law and medicine, in which the traditional division of labor between solicitors and barristers, or general practitioners and specialists, ostensibly serves the interests of the professionals rather than those of the clients. Whether these openly monopolistic arrangements hurt the interests of the public more than the more concealed, but not necessarily less effective, professional monopolies that exist elsewhere is an open question. They certainly formalize the elevated status of the professions and emphasize within the professions status differences of a kind that would not be tolerated in every society.

But behind the formalities of status distinctions, the English

---

[3] Those occupying the elite positions in higher education also possess university degrees, and have often been students of the *Ecole normale supérieure* as well.

system may be more liberal than either the French or the German one. The difference can be illustrated by the recruitment to higher civil service in England and France. In both countries selection is made on the basis of competitive examinations. But in France the jobs usually go to candidates who study at institutions that specially prepare for taking examinations, such as the *Ecole national d'administration,* the *Ecole libre des sciences politiques,* or tor some posts, the *Ecole polytechnique.* Students are selected for admission to these institutions by prior examinations that supposedly predict their ability to pass the examinations that follow. They may also have a university degree, but that does not necessarily imply that they have acquired specialized competence.

In England, civil service examinations require an honors degree from a university and are constructed to give equal chances to students with different disciplinary backgrounds. Therefore, the British civil servants are less a *preselected* elite than they are in France. They are trained in a variety of disciplines and, having succeeded in their special field of study in competition with colleagues, some of whom may subsequently become scholars, scientists, or lawyers, they can aspire to top positions in a civil service career. Therefore, the English civil servant will be more likely than his French counterpart to consider himself part of a class that includes professional people and to view himself as a professional person. This specialized educational background as a preparation for civil service was not unknown in Germany. But there civil servants were almost exclusively trained in the law faculties, and there were hierarchical differences dividing the academic elite from the civil service, and both of them from the "free" professions.

As a result, the status of Oxford and Cambridge and their predominance in training successful candidates for the civil service has not prevented the growth of either specialized disciplinary or intensive professional education at the universities. This contrasts with France, where all intensive university education has been stunted by the superiority of the *grandes écoles,* and with Germany, where intensive training for the professions was banned from the universities ruled by a privileged and socially insulated professorial estate.

In terms of stratification the English system has produced a continuous hierarchy within a unified professional class possessing common privileges but specialized expertise. The French system has produced primarily a mandarin class possessing special privileges in administering the country, and an intellectual class challenging the privileges of the elite and often critical of government and society in general. The British system is also less invidious than the German one, in which the academic and civil service elites have been insulated from the rest of the professions (Marshall, 1950, 44–47).

This juxtaposition may somewhat exaggerate the differences between these systems. There are also mandarins and intellectuals in England. Students who get into the best universities receive an education with a strong literary component. Those who succeed in civil service examinations and in subsequent careers in the civil service are very much like their French counterparts in background and outlook. There are also intellectuals, especially among university dons and students, who write and speak on a broad range of philosophical and general social concerns that are beyond their professional expertise. But the authority of the English mandarins and intellectuals is dependent on proven professional competence in some field and on their loyalty to the values of competence, objectivity, and responsibility of the professional class. They cannot afford to be just brilliant intellects or critics, as they can be in France. And they do not consider themselves a different breed from their erstwhile fellow students in other employment, as such intellectuals do in Germany.

PROFESSIONAL STUDIES IN THE UNITED STATES In the United States dissatisfaction with the classical curriculum and the poor standards of the colleges became acute only in the 1860s and the 1870s, more than 70 years later than it did in Europe. One of the reasons for this delay might have been the fact that higher education in the United States has been a less-public concern. The American college did not have a monopoly on training the professional elite in government service, and in medicine and law, as the continental European universities had, nor did it have a privileged connection with the ruling class and professional elite, as Oxford and Cambridge had in England. It could not have had such connections, since in the United States neither a ruling class nor a privileged professional elite existed. Only in its connection with the church were the American colleges comparable to the English universities, since a university degree was usually, though not in all denominations, a necessary condition of entry into the clergy. But even this close tie with some of the churches did not have the same meaning as it did in England, because there was no official state church in the United States. No colleges were supported by the federal government. Some were supported by the state, but the majority were private institutions with ties to different religious denominations. Their prestige depended on their reputations as character-forming educational institutions. Their educational ideal was the "Christian gentleman" (in the democratic American sense), not the scholar or the professional.

Therefore, the clash between privileged and underprivileged academics, or between intellectuals and professional people, was entirely absent from the background of American reform. The main participants of the reform movement were young scientists and scholars who had studied in Europe, mainly in Germany, and wanted to practice their new knowledge at home, and university and college presidents who sensed that there were new needs and opportunities for higher education and tried to identify and exploit them. While the scientists and scholars had some similarities with the European reformers, the college presidents had none. There were no private entrepreneurs in European higher education anywhere.

The German-trained scientists and scholars in the United States were thinking of an institution engaged primarily in disciplinary and selected professional studies, especially in medicine and law, in which research and training were closely integrated and in which advanced students were systematically trained for research. The university presidents were pragmatic people intent on finding and creating demand for higher education and on advancing the standing of their colleges. Education for the professions was a goal acceptable to both scholars and presidents: to the scholars, because according to the German model, professional training had to consist primarily of study and research in the basic disciplines; to the presidents, because demand for professional training was widespread and expected to grow. It was a market easy to develop since there were no facilities for advanced professional training in the United States, and those who wanted to obtain such training had to go to Europe (Veysey, 1965).

Indeed, education for the professions became one of the most distinct and by far the most influential of innovations of American higher education (Kerr, 1963, p. 18). Its evolution began with an attempt to implant the German model in the newly established Johns Hopkins University. This was planned to be purely a graduate school, engaged, more or less according to German examples, in the advanced training of students in the various arts and sciences and in medicine and law.

This was a challenge the other universities could not disregard. Once a single institution had committed itself to research and graduate education, the elite colleges had no choice but to follow suit. If they wanted to retain, or obtain, the services of competent scholars and scientists who would confer reputation on the college, they had to provide opportunities for research and for advanced teaching equal to those of their competitors. This meant establishing graduate programs in which scholars could teach how to do research.

However, while competition for scientists and scholars compelled the universities to establish graduate schools, competition for students compelled them to maintain their liberal arts programs. Eventually Johns Hopkins also had to establish a liberal arts program. But contrary to what had appeared to be the case in the beginning, these two enterprises turned out to be mutually supportive. The presidents of the prestigious colleges and universities—not to mention, of course, the less-prestigious ones—experimented with vocationally oriented bachelor's programs. The framework that made this experimentation possible was the elective program that allowed the student considerable choice among courses (Ben-David, 1972, pp. 87–94).

The presidents of these colleges subsequently opted for an overwhelmingly arts- and science-based liberal education after seeing that the vocationally oriented courses could not compete in interest or prestige. A course in English literature taught by someone who knew the subject well was bound to appeal to more students than a course in accountancy, even if the latter was taught well. Therefore, the liberal arts course managed to retain its dominance, especially in institutions that attracted able and relatively well-to-do students who were not too anxious about the immediate payoff of their studies. This is not to say that all these students were interested in a liberal education as an end in itself. The elective system makes possible a considerable degree of preprofessional specialization within the liberal arts program, and a majority of liberal arts students consider their studies a preparation for specialized professional studies in graduate school.[4]

In any event, the success of the modernized liberal arts course also ensured the success of the graduate school, which in the beginning had to make great efforts to attract students. Teachers in the arts and sciences had to be trained for up-to-date undergraduate liberal arts programs, and the demand for such teachers spurred the growth of graduate schools. In the humanities and social sciences, and to a somewhat lesser extent also in the natural sciences, Ph.D. programs developed as professional training programs for teachers in colleges and universities.

Thus as far as the arts and sciences are concerned, the integration of research with teaching took place in the United States quite unlike the way it had in Germany, which served as the model for this integration. In Germany the integration meant that all students intending to study arts and sciences were taught disciplinary courses suited for specialists by teacher-researchers. Allowances for differences in the kinds and levels of the educational goals of the students were made by a permissive educational regime. This system allowed some students to be trained in research and others to acquire varying degrees of erudition in their specialized field. In the United States integration of research and teaching meant that students of arts and sciences were taught preferably by competent, professionally trained researcher-teachers. But there was one framework for the training of professional research workers—the graduate school, especially that of the arts and sciences—and another— the liberal arts college—for teaching these disciplines as a background for, or introduction to, further professional studies, or as a means of general education. The graduate school became a professional school for researchers in which research apprenticeship was an integral part of the training. In the liberal arts course, research has been only a background of or a didactic complement to the studies. Teaching is intensive at this level, too, but is adapted to the different purposes of the students.

A similar relationship has emerged between research, teach-

[4] According to a study made in 1961, 76 percent of college seniors intended to go on to professional or graduate school (Davis, 1965, p. 201).

ing, and practical training in the so-called professional schools. I say "so-called" because, as has been pointed out, the graduate school of arts and sciences also provides professional education. Professional schools too, have eventually sorted themselves into essentially two kinds of institutions: those that include a major element of research in their programs, and those that do not. Until the Second World War no professional education invariably integrated training with research. Some schools placed very little emphasis on research even in medicine, which had the most tightly regulated training requirements of any profession and an advanced degree, the M.D., as the minimal qualification for practice. Those that did not emphasize research tended to turn out practitioners, while those that did primarily trained medical researchers, teachers, and specialists for medical schools and training hospitals. The emphasis on research in other professions corresponded more or less to the level of their degree program. First professional degrees had been, and still are, highly vocational and practical, with the exception of some first degrees in engineering that have actually been of a second-degree level; training at the master's level may have been slightly more research oriented, but only in Ph.D.-level programs has professional training been invariably integrated with research. Thus research and teaching are integrated in the arts and sciences essentially the same way as in the professional studies. Integration in both instances takes place through Ph.D. programs, which have a monopoly in the training of teachers for all degree levels. But this has not reduced the number of professional training schemes. Nor has it led to a diminution of the intensity of training at all levels and of all types. The varieties of professional training in the American system are greater than those even in Britain, not to speak of the other European countries (except in some fields in the U.S.S.R.). Some of them stress thorough mastery of the scientific basis, and may include experience in advanced research. Others are more practically oriented, and some are no more than courses for high-level technicians. But irrespective of the level and type of the program, the universities accept responsibility (as in England) for imparting practical competence commensurate with the program. In no case have universities the option of French and German universities of contenting themselves with the general education of the professionals in the basic fields and leaving the acquisition of practical experience to the graduate or his employer or to both. The reason for this is that initially American universities had no monopoly on professional training and could not have attracted students without giving them a training of practical value. The degree had to be a marketable product with good specifications. Therefore, one could, and still can, make a fairly valid inference about the competence of a graduate from the level and field of his or her degree and from the institution that conferred the degree.

The responsibility for the practical training of the student, and the existence of a hierarchy of recognized professional training, are both much more reminiscent of the English system than of the German one. Local traditions and circumstances deriving from England and Scotland were in these respects more powerful than the implanted German model. But both elements developed in the United States far beyond the British precedents.

Greater responsibility for practical training is evident in the complete incorporation of apprenticeship training in the regular university program. The division of labor that existed in England between the basic medical departments forming an integral part of the universities and the practically autonomous teaching hospitals in charge of clinical training, or between the legal teaching at the university and apprenticeship at the office of a solicitor or a barrister, has not been accepted in the United States. The idea that professional training was to be shared by universities and professional associations has been by and large absent.

The American system developed a unity and hierarchy in professional training and professional university degrees that had been almost entirely absent from the English system. In England the professional hierarchy was maintained primarily through degrees and titles conferred by the professional associations, and not by different degrees. Finally, the American hierarchy confers the highest academic prestige on the Ph.D. programs. The best institutions and the best departments, including the best professional departments, have increasingly devoted themselves to training researchers. This is not to say that other types of training are not done intensively and effectively, but within the academic system they have lost prestige compared to the Ph.D. program. This is very different from the

British professional tradition which has only recently, under American influence, begun to stress research.

The hierarchy of academic functions placing the Ph.D. program on the top developed in the absence of firmly established elite institions. Originally, the most prestigious universities, including Harvard, had tried to maintain the prestige of their liberal arts curriculum independent from the graduate program. Like Oxford and Cambridge in England, or the elite *grandes écoles* in France, they were of the view that the training of future civil servants, businessmen, politicians, and elite professionals was no less a mission than the training of scientists and scholars. But the prestige of the American elite universities had not been conferred on them by the state or by custom. As in Germany, it was based on their educational excellence and success in recruiting the most desirable students. In maintaining their privilege, they had to compete with serious challengers, such as John Hopkins, Chicago, Berkeley, Wisconsin, and Michigan. In this competition the ability to attract the best scholars has been the most important long-term factor. Since scholars are attracted by research and graduate training, the ascendancy of the Ph.D. programs was inevitable.

The combined result of the incorporation of practical training and the ascendancy of the doctoral programs has been the emergence of Ph.D. programs (and research) in professional fields that did not have much of a theoretical content. Those who taught the practical aspects of the professions needed doctoral degrees to establish their academic credentials and to promote the academic standing of their field. In such a field as medicine this did not present a serious problem, since the clinical fields had sufficient disciplinary, or theoretical, content to make research possible at a reasonable level.

But in newer fields, like education, business, public administration, and perhaps also in some fields of engineering, it was not easy to find academic disciplines directly related to practice. Nevertheless, doctoral programs have been established on many occasions prior to the existence of significant research to force-feed research and thus to introduce methods and principles to a practical tradition in search of professional status (Flexner, 1930, pp. 54–72, 96–124).

These practices have lent to the "professionalization" of occupations and to professional education a peculiar and precise meaning that they had not had before. The basis of professionalization is the existence of both basic disciplinary and practical problem-oriented research focused on a given professional field and a Ph.D. program based on such research. The rank and file of the profession are trained either on the first- or (more usually) on the second-degree level by teachers preferably possessing Ph.D. degrees in the professional field, according to a program that includes study of the basic disciplines and supervised practical training. This conception of professions combined the logic of the German academic system, which distinguished professions from other occupations by their scientific content, with the British tradition that regarded professional training as the acquisition of a high degree of competence and trustworthiness in a technically or institutionally complex and/or publicly "important" field.

Speaking in merely evolutionary terms, American professional training has been far more "successful" than the others. It has produced a larger and more differentiated professional class than has emerged in the other countries. It has avoided the pitfall, apparent in both the French and German systems, of creating an unchanging core of intensively trained elite professionals and a superficially educated and partly wasted periphery of poorly trained professionals, dropouts, perpetual students, and alienated intellectuals. It has also overcome the intellectual rigidity of the purely pragmatic, technique-oriented, practical training customary in England by adopting a very flexible notion of research as the basis of all professional education. It has also gone further than any of the European systems in eliminating elements based on traditional status distinctions—such as the elevated status of those possessing academic degrees in continental Europe, or of membership in prestigious professional associations in England—from professionalism.

This explains the attractiveness of American professional education and the attempts to imitate it all over the world. This is not to say, however, that it is a perfect, or even the best possible, type of professional education.

The American system developed at a time when the universities had to show impressive results of practical value in order to establish themselves in a society that did not recognize their monopoly on professional training. Once the exclusive privilege of the university to confer professional degrees has been established, there is plenty of room for its abuse. Occupational groups in search of such privilege can bring pressure on state universities, or seduce private ones, into establishing professional training schemes and degrees in fields in which research contributes nothing either to the advancement of knowledge or to practice. Such degrees then can be used to create closed shops in some fields of employment without any improvement in the standards of service. In fact, professionalization may depress standards by substituting useless quasi-scientific doctrine for useful tradition, common sense, and trial and error.

Some mechanisms in the American university system reduce the likelihood of such harmful consequences. Abraham Flexner (1930, pp. 54–72, 94–124) had thought that schools of business and schools of education in the 1920s represented such harmful trends. But business schools had no chance whatever to establish a monopoly of their graduates in higher positions in business. Therefore, they had to continue experimenting and producing research and graduates who were recognized as useful by business. In education, collusion between universities, professional associations, and local governments was possible because education is a monopolistic service and local educational systems do not have to prove themselves in competition. But there have been some checks on monopoly even in this field. Educational research and training has been subjected to criticism by the academic community as well as by politicians, and the existence of different local educational authorities in the near vicinity of each other has provided some check on abuse of professional monopoly. But these are largely external checks on the system. Internally, a system like American professional education is prone to deterioration of standards. This is an important consideration when using it as a model for other countries where similar external checks may not exist.

THE REFORM OF PROFESSIONAL EDUCATION The development of professional education in the four countries compared in this chapter can be viewed as a sequence of interrelated attempts to reform professional education. The official goals of these attempts were to abolish the status privileges of the old professions of theology, law, and medicine; concomitantly, to sever their ties with the privileged classes of society bent on monopolizing for themselves the services of the intellectually and educationally most competent groups in society; and to replace classical learning as the common basis of all professional learning with new specialized programs directly relevant to professional performance.

The background of these attempts was the loss of faith in classical learning as a source of true knowledge that resulted from the rise of modern science and the new philosophy of Enlightenment based on this science. People began to look forward, discovering new and ever-improving knowledge through research, not backward by searching for it in ancient books. With this loss of the charisma of classical learning, gone was the basis of the status privileges of the professional class possessing such learning. As has been pointed out, the professional class itself neglected classical learning and contented itself with only a semblance of it.

The situation seemed to provide an opportunity for the abolishment of all professional privilege. Modern science and technology did not seem to provide a basis for the rise of a professional class. Scientific and technological knowledge is specialized, and it would logically create a variety of specialists rather than a unified class of learned professionals. Furthermore, the specificity and instrumental character of scientific and technological knowledge seemed to be inconsistent with ascriptive status privilege. It was assumed that such knowledge would have practical effects that the clients could judge for themselves, so that formal degrees and other status privileges would lose their importance. The charisma of this knowledge would be dispersed and manifested in the actual work done by people who possessed and used it, and not concentrated in a status group.

Actually, as has been seen, professional privilege has reemerged, in spite of the great expansion of opportunities for the acquisition of professional qualifications in a variety of fields. In France scientific technological knowledge was used to a large extent not as a preparation for practical work, but as a means of selection for the hierarchy of a new mandarin class. Achievement in research became the basis of high academic status in Germany; nevertheless, there too the system developed into a highly formalized hierarchy. There was no real dispersal of charisma, since those who did not become researchers did not receive an effective training, and very often their principal aim was to obtain a degree that—as in France—conferred on them an essentially ascriptive status. Since the source of this status was the university, this system of ascriptive statuses contaminated also the achievement-based status of the professor. His title and honors were more conspicuous than his specific achievement.

Only Britain and the United States developed a flexible and continuous gradation in professional prestige based on criteria of achievement. Training for each profession at every level became intensive and led to the acquisition of practical competence at the appropriate level. This has gradually eliminated the old ascriptive elements of professional status, but has given rise to opportunities for the emergence of new ones. Universities and academic teacher-researchers have attained a position of monopoly in awarding professional status. The position of academic teacher-researchers today is comparable to that of the erstwhile humanistically trained teaching clergy as the core profession that unites and lends legitimacy to the professional system as a whole. This is not to say that this new core profession is comparable to the clergy in other respects. Unlike the clergy, it is a highly specialized and differentiated group, and it has never sought to base its authority on unchanging doctrine or to bolster its doctrines through governmental coercion. Thus monopoly is not unchecked, and the possibility of abuse is limited, but there are temptations to abuse this monopoly for the creation of new professional privilege insufficiently supported by scientific and technological knowledge. Such abuse would not create a small, parasitical professional upper class, but instead large, parasitical professional lower and middle classes using academic credentialism for the creation of perhaps even more harmful monopolies than that of the traditional higher professions.

CONCLUSION The new credentialism is a serious threat to higher education. If its spread is unchecked, it will empty scientific professionalism of its contents and undermine its charisma. But the situation is far from being parallel to that which led to the demise of the old professionalism based on classical learning. In the eighteenth and nineteenth centuries there was a serious competitor to classical learning, namely, modern science. Now there is no competitor in sight, and therefore the problem is how to prevent abuse of professionalism and increase the efficiency of professional training, rather than to replace it with something else.

The prospects for such positive development are not bad. In spite of the weaknesses and vulnerabilities of the different systems, the overall development in education for the professions has been a considerable success. Professional education has become increasingly scientific. New conceptions of professional training have been rapidly diffused, although institutional means have not always been adequate to realize them. As has been seen, continental European systems are not well adapted to training for the variety of new professions; the training obtained in them is often not sufficiently intensive; and the European professionalism still contains elements of old privilege. But for the student capable of initiative there are good opportunities for training everywhere through combinations of study and individual apprenticeship. The aim of subsequent university reforms in Europe and the United States throughout the nineteenth century, to create a new scientific and technological basis for professional education, has been realized.

This cannot be said of the idea—particularly pronounced among many French and German reformers—that all higher education would become specialized professional education. Liberal education has survived in the United States, and elements of a general education are implicit in the other systems. Furthermore, research, originally conceived both in France and Germany as a private activity of professors and a few advanced students, and in Germany also as serving as a basis for teaching students specializing in different professional fields, has become an increasingly independent university function. Thus while university reform has, indeed, transformed professional training, it has also had effects and led to the development of further functions that were not foreseen by the early reformers. We turn now to these unforeseen functions of general education and research.

4. General Higher Education

In spite of their predominantly professional purpose, systems of higher education contain conceptions of what higher education is in general, beyond the instrumental requirements of the careers for which it prepares. In France and in Germany— which have not had university programs in general education since the early nineteenth century—these conceptions are implicit in the educational practices of the universities; in Britain and especially in the United States they are explicit. In the United States there is also a distinct and important general educational program, the liberal arts course, and in Britain there are several programs providing this kind of education.[1] These different conceptions have been outlined in the previous chapter. In this one they will be spelled out in more detail.

FRANCE AND GERMANY The contents of French higher education, as has been seen, are not highly specialized. Until the 1880s the *licence* in arts (*licence ès lettres*) involved no specialization, and there was little specialization in science, either. Subsequently education in the arts and sciences gradually became more specialized and was accompanied by constant concern for a good grounding in classical studies and language and, in the natural sciences, for mathematics. Even education at an engineering school like the *Ecole polytechnique* is broad, stressing such basics as mathematics and theoretical physics much more than experimental science, and including courses in economics, philosophy, and literature. As has been pointed out, this concern with breadth and with general verbal and logical skills is also characteristic of the system of examinations.

[1] For example, in the University of Sussex (Organisation for Economic Co-operation and Development, 1972, pp. 237–242).

Nevertheless, the aim of this system is to prepare students for examinations qualifying them for specific professional careers. Thus the general, nonspecialized nature of the arts course is related to the fact that the large majority of arts students prepare for careers as teachers in high school, the purpose of which is to provide a good general education based on the mastery of French and on a good grounding in the classics. Nor does a general practitioner in medicine, or a managing director in a state-owned tobacco factory, require highly specialized knowledge. They require a good general grasp of their field and the ability and the intellectual tools to acquire such knowledge when needed. The task of the educational and licensing institutions—which in France are the same—is to make sure that the candidate has this ability and has acquired these tools.

In the French conception these tools, as well as the ability to use them, are fairly general. According to this conception there are some differences between the intellectual ability of the humanistically and the mathematically inclined, and there is a corresponding division between the educational traditions based on verbal and mathematical logic; but essentially a few general subjects, such as grammar, rhetoric, logic, and mathematics, are considered the basis of all specialized knowledge. Therefore, for a long time there was no sharp division between the lycées and the faculties of arts and sciences. The same professors might serve in both institutions, and the *licence* and the *agrégation* were in a way just more advanced *baccalauréats;* they required essentially the same kind of knowledge, only at a higher level of mastery.

Thus there was a great deal of continuity between the contents of general and professional education. The students in the lycées studied in order to develop their mental and moral character; those at the faculties of arts and sciences—the *Ecole normale supérieure* or the *Ecole polytechnique*—studied in order to use their knowledge in their careers as teachers or members of other professions. But they studied the same things at different levels on a relatively unified scale of intellectual and educational excellence. This conception of an essentially single scale of educational excellence is still widespread in France. Perhaps it is no longer dominant in the sense that a majority of people actually believe in it, or that educational practice is guided by it, but it has not been replaced by any other conception. There are those who accept the concept and those who oppose it, but those who oppose it are not sure what to substitute for it.

This is in sharp contrast to the German approach, which makes a qualitative distinction between general and higher education. General education has been relegated since the beginning of the nineteenth century to the *Gymnasien*, and has consisted more or less of the same things as in France, namely, language, literature, history (both modern and classic), mathematics, physics, and some chemistry and biology. This knowledge is considered a necessary precondition of higher education, but different from it in kind. Higher education is the acquisition of specialized competence leading up to and preferably beyond the frontiers of knowledge through original research. No degree of intellectual virtuosity or breadth of knowledge can be considered a sign of higher education if it is unaccompanied by the exploration of new problems through research.

These are fundamentally different conceptions of the general element in higher education. In France it is conceived of as virtuosity in handling well-defined intellectual contents. In Germany it is the intellectual experience of original discovery, irrespective of the contents in which it is made.

As has been pointed out, the French conception implies a great deal of continuity between the academic secondary education and higher education, while the German system postulates discontinuity between the two. As a result French higher education was extremely reluctant to specialize, while in Germany there was a pressure to specialize secondary education by the middle of the nineteenth century (Paulsen, 1921, pp. 544–637; Zeldin, 1967, pp. 64–65).

A common element in both traditions is the assumption that higher education is a means for the selection and education of an intellectual elite. The difference between the two systems has been in strategy. The French system tries to select its specialists by identifying their general intellectual qualities; the German one attempts to select its elite by observing success in the study of scholarly and scientific specialties. But though one emphasizes general education and the other scientific preparation, both systems are devised to educate a select minority who combine intellectual leadership with a career in academic life, the civil service, or the professions.

But–except in the French *grandes écoles*—none of these conceptions have been consistently realized in practice because the assumptions behind them have been unrealistic. In every country of continental Europe since the end of the nineteenth century large numbers of students have gone to the university to improve their education and their chances in life without a specific career or discipline in mind. Since the system of higher education did not cater to such needs, the students had to choose what would most help them fulfill their expectations. In the majority of the countries this was the study of law, combined with some political science and economics. These were relatively undemanding and not very technical studies (economics was usually of the descriptive institutional type, rather than of the analytical-mathematical one), which dealt with matters of general human interest, and they prepared students for a relatively broad range of occupations in the civil service and in the administration of private business (Zeldin, 1967, p. 64).

This "general education" by default was not a satisfactory solution to the problems of this kind of student. Many students did not take their studies seriously because they chose them only in the absence of anything suited to their purpose, and the teachers and the university authorities tolerated the situation because they assumed that those who actually wanted to practice a profession (especially law) would have to pass further qualifying examinations. However, it was a mistake to believe that such corruption of the functions of the university would not have undesirable consequences. The large numbers of frustrated students became a breeding ground of political and moral unrest and irresponsibility. Their poor education, coupled with high but frustrated expectations, probably further diminished their chances of finding satisfactory work. This gave rise to an intellectualism that became identified with unemployability, economic frustration, and political radicalism, rather than with an increased competence in work and a capacity to enjoy leisure. Therefore, the growth of higher education was considered a liability rather than an asset to society. Intellectuals were considered a problem, and governments vacillated between suppressing them or bribing them by creating unnecessary bureaucratic jobs for their employment (Kotschnig, 1937; Mannheim, 1944, pp. 98–114; Ringer, 1969, p. 65; Schumpeter, 1947, pp. 145–155; Zeldin, 1967, p. 67).

ENGLAND The English universities, unlike their continental counterparts, were private institutions that served distinct client groups. The two oldest and most prestigious ones, Oxford and Cambridge, educated the sons of the aristocracy and those intending to enter the clergy and the learned professions. The new institutions of higher education competed with Oxford and Cambridge in educating professionals, but had little chance of competing in the education of the upper classes or the clergy, who were still an important force in the nineteenth century. Therefore, the old universities were reluctant to abandon the task of educating a general gentlemanly class and to take on an overwhelmingly professional education. There was strong advocacy to retain, albeit in an improved form, the humanistic ideal of general liberal education.

Eventually, the ancient universities were reformed mainly, as has been seen, according to the German model, but they insisted, much more truthfully than the German universities ever could, that the purpose of specialized study was not necessarily the acquisition of practical skills, but that it was the best way to the education of the mind and was an end in itself. This insistence enabled them to maintain the ideal of a liberal education that had no direct orientation to careers, and at the same time recruit as teachers competent scientists and scholars who were, of course, specialists and "professionals" in their fields. Thus the distinction between the general education ideal of creating an intellectual elite and the preparation of students for professional positions, which was purely theoretical in the French and the German systems, here became at least a partial reality. Some students at Oxford and Cambridge could afford to and actually did study on a seriously specialized level for the general educational purpose of improving their minds, without having any specific career in mind (see above, p. 23). Probably because of the relative success of the elite universities in this kind of education, there has been little insistence in England to perpetuate the disjunction between the "general" education of the secondary schools and the specialized education of the universities. The sixth form of the grammar school (that is, the upper division of the academically oriented high school) has become fairly specialized, though allowing a wide range of choice in subjects, and has virtually abandoned the idea of a common general educational content. Thus English secondary education adopted the idea of general education of the mind through the study of a limited number of fields in depth, rather than through the acquisition of a standard range of traditionally prescribed content—an idea that has never been officially adopted in German secondary education (and in France hardly at all, even in higher education).

However, in spite of the idea that specialized education can also serve general educational purposes, specialization undertaken largely for a practical professional purpose has become overwhelmingly the end of university education in England. But British universities (and here I include the Scottish ones) have effectively resisted the transformation of certain specialties into "soft options" taken for general educational purposes. Admission to British universities has never depended solely on passing examinations devised by authorities other than the universities, and the universities have been relatively successful in adjusting their admissions requirements to their ability to train students effectively and to place them in careers commensurate to their training. As a result the British system has been relatively immune to corruption and unrest and to the problems of intellectual unemployment and underemployment endemic to the continental systems (Kotschnig, 1937).

The general educational purpose has also not declined as completely in Britain as on the Continent. It is still possible to obtain a nonspecialized "pass degree," although this is not a degree the universities want to confer. But certain universities experiment in new, high-standard, liberal-arts-type, first-degree programs, and other universities in programs based on a wide range of electives (Organisation for Economic Co-operation and Development, 1972, pp. 237–242).

Even universities that prefer specialized curricula feel some responsibility for the general intellectual and moral education of their students. Universities have tried to maintain student residences with some educational supervision and have organized individual tutorships. Students are often advised to read and write about topics outside their specialties, and there is active concern with their progress in their specialized studies as well as with their educational and personal development in general. Thus, in addition to specialized competence, university education has also more or less explicitly served to improve the mind and the character of the student in general. And, what is most important, it has been considered successful in this respect. The university-educated person has always been considered an asset in employment (in or outside the sphere of his specialized competence) as well as in political and other public activity. Graduates were considered an elite because they were fairly well selected and educated, not because possessors of academic degrees enjoyed formal privileges and traditional prestige. Since they were actually well selected and educated, they also did not have serious problems in employment.

ABANDONMENT OF LIBERAL EDUCATION
The reason that English universities by and large eliminated general education from the curricula despite its importance to them seems to have been that, from the point of view of the academic teachers, providing a solid general education is, and has been since the late eighteenth century, an almost impossible task. As has been seen, there are basic disagreements about what should constitute such an education. For those who define higher education as study combined with research, a general higher educational curriculum is a self-contradiction. And those who can conceive of higher education without a significant element of research have found it increasingly difficult to specify the range and variety of studies to be included in such education. Furthermore, the creation of a general educational curriculum requires planning, coordination, and organization. This implies some authoritative bureaucratic supervision, something that university professors have always found restrictive and distasteful. In the continental European universities, which have been guilds of independent professors representing different specialties rather than bureaucratic organizations, there has been simply no authority to create such courses of study. To do so would involve a drastic change in the character and organization of the universities.

Only the French *grandes écoles* have the organization for such a program, and indeed they have curricula integrated across disciplines. But the better scholars and scientists have moved to universities in which instruction is much less structured by administrative directive, giving rise to the absurdity of the best scholars and scientists teaching in a liberal manner the less able students, while the best students are taught by a lower grade of teachers and study under much stricter supervision.

The British universities were administratively somewhat better integrated than the European ones. They made no artificial separation between responsibility for university plants and finances on the one hand, and for teaching and research on the other. In continental Europe, the former was a bureaucratic responsibility of central or state governments, while the latter was a prerogative of academic teachers corporately safeguarding their individual academic freedom from interference by outsiders or by one another. In England the Oxford and Cambridge colleges were real self-governing bodies, responsible for their own finances and for a common educational policy as well as for all other aspects of their operations, which were supported to a large extent by student fees (until the 1930s).[2] Thus they had to pay attention to the welfare and education of the students who, unlike students in continental Europe, were not attracted to the universities by the inexpensive study. But the British universities were teachers' universities in the sense that professors (or at Oxford and Cambridge, the dons) had an overwhelming influence on their administration. The creation of an up-to-date curriculum composed of studies in a large variety of fields would have required a degree of consensus among teachers in remote disciplines, and cooperation between them, that could not be attained. This explains why the liberal educational curriculum was abandoned in spite of the retention of the aim of a general, non-career-oriented higher education.

LIBERAL EDUCATION IN THE UNITED STATES The matter of student fees and the nature of academic government also helps to understand why both the aim and the contents of a liberal education have been retained in the United States. There the college was originally a private educational institution, run by a president rather than by groups of professors or tutors. Parents paid a reasonable fee for tuition, and the president was personally responsible for effective education. He hired the professors, who, originally, were only his helpers. Max Weber, the great German sociologist who visited the United States near the end of the period of university reform (in 1904), wrote: "The American student's conception of the teacher who faces him is: he sells me his knowledge and his methods for my father's money" (in Gerth & Mills, 1946, p.

---

[2] Student fees accounted for up to about 30 percent of their income. Other private sources, such as endowments and donations, constituted an additional 15 to 18 percent (see Halsey & Trow, 1971, p. 63).

149). The role and the authority of the president have changed since then, but it is still true that colleges "sell" a certain kind of education and employ teachers according to the needs of an overall, coordinated educational program.

Therefore, in contrast to Europe (including Britain) a general higher education in the United States was organizationally feasible. The framework and authority to create and coordinate such a *curriculum* existed. Furthermore, the demand for such an education, which existed also in Europe, was even more articulated in the United States. The middle classes were interested in giving their children a higher education, were capable and willing to pay the full cost of such education (at least the full cost of current expenditure on teaching), and were much larger and stronger than in Europe. And since they either paid themselves, or controlled the state legislatures that paid for education, their wishes had to be heeded.

But an intellectual tradition also facilitated the maintenance of a program of general higher education even after the late nineteenth-century reform of American universities. This was the partial reformation of the American college in the eighteenth century under the impact of the Scottish universities, which were then the most advanced institutions of higher education in the world (Sloan, 1971, pp.23–32). Scotland was in the eighteenth century the most important provincial center of Enlightenment philosophy and science. Scottish philosophers, like the French ones, believed that a philosophical unity underlay all science and scholarship, and believed in the intellectual value of scientific and other modern studies. But their philosophies were more inductive and less abstract than those of their French counterparts, and their educational schemes contained much empirical science and scholarship. Another important difference between them and eighteenth-century French philosophers was their attitude toward religion. In Scotland, philosophy could live together with religion under terms acceptable to both sides. This made possible the reform of the universities without revolution and governmental decrees, and the trying out of the new educational ideas in practice. Thus the idea so central to continental European reformers, to replace the universities with specialized institutions, never took hold in Scotland. The reform of the universities had begun in the first half of the eighteenth century and was well advanced by mid-century, before the idea of replacing universities with specialized institutions became generally accepted. Francis Hutcheson gave his philosophy lectures at Glasgow in 1730 in English, and soon English became the main language of instruction everywhere. Specialized professorships were introduced in all Scottish universities; there was considerable openness toward new fields of science and scholarship, practical or applied; and old scholastic logic and metaphysics were replaced by courses in new philosophy that—in the Enlightenment manner—tried to synthesize the results of modern science and apply them to the traditional questions of philosophy. With the possible exception of Göttingen and Halle, in Germany, this was much in advance of what was attained by even the most radical reforms of "enlightened" rulers in Europe, such as Maria Theresia and Joseph II, the Austrian emperors, in the second half of the century (Paulsen, 1921, pp. 109–113, 126–148).

For reasons that have not yet been explored, the Scottish universities were not able to maintain their scientific momentum. Perhaps their reform was premature in the sense that the new subjects could not yet effectively compete with classical learning, so that they remained ultimately peripheral subjects. Another reason might have been the attempt at a philosophical synthesis of all the studies, a chimerical dream of Enlightenment philosophy that also failed in France. The new scientific studies as educational disciplines requiring specialization were successful in Germany because the philosophers failed to impose their wish on the universities. The Scottish philosophers were more successful, but the cost of their success may have been the relative decline of science at their universities. Nevertheless, the Scottish universities, unlike their English counterparts, were reformed institutions by the middle of the eighteenth century. Even if their scientific and scholarly excellence diminished, they were institutions that took account of the spirit of modern science and were probably quite effective in their efforts to impart a modern world view to their students.

The prereform nineteenth-century American college was in many ways a provincial replica of Scottish antecedents (Sloan, 1971, p. 245). It had never had any of the scientific excellence of the eighteenth-century Scottish universities, and it had much more serious religious commitments. Its curriculum was meager and of low quality, and the innovations imported from

Scotland became sterile educational orthodoxy. But the philosophy of the American colleges was post-Enlightenment Scottish philosophy, which tried to mediate between science and religion. The moral philosophy course, usually taught by the college president to the senior-year students, was a kind of modern philosophy cum eighteenth-century social science and was open, at least in principle, to scientific and modern professional subjects. This is not to say that the tradition would have been capable of rejuvenating itself without external influence. That did not happen either in Scotland or in the United States. But when the German influence of specialized science was imported into the United States, the liberal arts college was capable of absorbing it without diverting from general education. The American college had a framework and a purpose that were partly modern. All it needed was a new content to lend substance to this purpose.

This content seemed to be the specialized sciences and technologies that had developed in the nineteenth century. But how this new knowledge could be absorbed into the universities was not evident. The original idea of Charles Eliot, the president of Harvard, and of Andrew White, the president of newly founded Cornell, was to introduce the new fields as electives, thus diversifying the existing curriculum. Alone, this idea would probably not have worked. It would not have been possible to find competent teachers, or to teach isolated courses in different subjects to a student body with a heterogeneous educational background. Thus difficult problems in integrating these studies would have arisen. These problems were resolved by another aspect of the reform initiated at other universities (although Eliot also took part in this), namely, the establishment of the graduate school.

As was pointed out in the previous chapter, the original purpose of this reform undertaken in the 1870s under the influence of German ideas was not the improvement of liberal arts education but its replacement with specialized higher education. However, because there were no central organizations (even to the extent that there were in England) to mastermind the changes and to pay out of public funds for services that might not have been in demand, the liberal arts college survived. Johns Hopkins University, which was founded in 1876 as a purely specialized graduate school, did not have quite the same effect on American higher education as the establishment of the University of Berlin in 1810 had on German higher education. Although Johns Hopkins was a great success scientifically, it was far less successful economically. Parents were willing to pay for a college education, but the demand for advanced scientific or even professional education was much more limited. The success of the graduate school required a demand for its services, and that could come only when other types of higher education (especially the liberal arts college) improved. The liberal arts college was also the most obvious place of employment for scholars trained at graduate schools in the arts and sciences. But for that purpose the college had to be reformed and its curriculum expanded so that it would be able to utilize the variety of specialists trained at the graduate schools. The partially laissez faire, free-market approach to the liberal arts college curriculum in the elective system made such reform possible. Students could choose their courses and compose their own curricula within broad limits. Concomitantly, student demand induced the colleges to extend their range of offerings. For example:

At Harvard in 1870–71, there were 643 undergraduate students and 73 courses offered by 32 professors. In 1910–11, the corresponding figures were 2,217 students, 401 courses, and 169 professors. At Yale College, between the years 1870 and 1910, the number of students increased from 522 to 1,519 and the number of teachers from 19 to 192. The development at Princeton was similar. Between the years 1870 and 1910, the number of students increased from 361 to 1,301, and the number of teachers from 18 to 174. This shows that while the number of students during this period of the introduction of electives grew about threefold in these three institutions, the number of teachers increased from five to tenfold due to the introduction of new types of courses (Ben-David, 1972, p. 57).

Thus the reform of the undergraduate curriculum created a demand for teachers trained in the graduate schools. College reform was, therefore, as much a condition of the success of the graduate schools as the reform of the German *Gymnasien* in the early nineteenth century and their subsequent need for teachers was a condition of the success of the reformed German universities. But there was also an obverse relationship that is usually overlooked but that is no less important: namely, that the establishment of graduate schools as extensions of colleges made possible the modernization of the liberal arts curriculum. As has been pointed out, the general program of higher education foundered even in Britain, where there was a positive predisposition toward it, and in France, where much of the reformed professional education had been based on general educational curricula, because science and scholarship became so specialized that first-rate scholars were not willing to teach courses in a program of general education. In the United States a scholar could train his graduate students up to his own level, and yet participate in a general program for undergraduates. Thus what could not succeed in Europe, where universities actually taught for a single degree (preparation for the higher degrees was usually informal), could succeed in the United States because, although graduate and undergraduate training were differentiated, the new graduate-level education was kept in institutions that also provided education for undergraduates.

This system also solved to some extent the problem of selecting and integrating electives. The graduate schools could lay down standards for courses and could determine which electives were acceptable for course sequences.

But it did not solve the two interrelated problems of how the curriculum as a whole should be composed and what the educational goal of this general curriculum should be. These problems do not have a single and permanent solution. Students have different problems and different goals in life, and, accordingly, they need different kinds of general education. Besides, personal goals as well as the contents of science and scholarship change in ways that are much more difficult to take into account in general than in specialized education. Therefore, asking these questions (as they are usually formulated in educational literature) is somewhat misleading. The practical problem is how to create curricula that meet the needs of all the variety of students admitted to a college (of course, no college can responsibly admit everyone) and how to ensure ongoing revision and updating of the curricula. This means a quest for an educational strategy as much as for finding alternative educational contents, rather than selecting a given dogma of general education and determining the contents accordingly.[3]

[3] This statement applies mainly to systems of higher education. A single institution, especially a small one, may be justified to settle on a given dogma. But given the progressive character of modern learning, even such institutions need strategies for the frequent review and possible change of their dogmas.

The elective system constituted such a strategy. As originally conceived, it was a broad range of offerings that allowed students to fit their studies to vocational, preprofessional, and general educational purposes. Eventually the vocational purpose was separated from the liberal arts college program because, to be effective, it required more practical work and a different type of teacher compared with the other courses. But colleges have continued to cater to students with a variety of purposes, such as those who use college as a preparation for graduate studies in a specific field (such as medicine or mathematics), those who use it as a place in which to get acquainted with a variety of specialized endeavors and to choose from them one for graduate study, and, finally, those who regard college as their terminal education and as a means to further their intellectual and psychological maturation.

The education of the first group has never presented particular problems. Colleges attached to universities have always had the means and the motivation to educate students of this type. Their only problem has been to set the appropriate breadth requirements for such students, and this problem allows a variety of solutions.

But the other two types of students require more than good courses. They need guidance in integrating their studies and choosing a meaningful goal. Teachers competent in a special field rarely have the ability or the motivation to perform these tasks. This requires educators and ways of coordinating courses that are difficult to achieve. However, all the colleges have a range of guidance and counseling services that work at least for the second type of student, who comes to college to make an intellectual and professional choice.

The most difficult problem has been presented by the students who come to college in order to mature or to "find themselves." Both of these aims have an intellectual and a moral aspect. Even if no explicitly moral problems were involved in such education, and the college had only to choose for such students a meaningful combination of courses, the choice itself would involve value judgments of a kind that do not exist in setting program requirements for students who know what they are studying for, or for those who do not yet have, but who expect to have, a specific intellectual and vocational purpose after finding out at college what best suits their abilities and opportunities.

American colleges have handled this problem of education for a general purpose in different ways. Many of them experimented at different times with integrated curricula that reflected the intellectual and moral values of those who constructed the curricula. The effectiveness of these attempts varied a great deal depending on the quality of students and teachers and their acceptance of the values on which the given curriculum was based. Because of these variables, none of these attempts (the best known of which were made at Columbia University during the First World War, at the University of Chicago in the 1930s, and at Harvard University in the 1940s) lasted, and none of them became generally or even widely accepted.

The colleges were successful in keeping together and educating this diverse and increasingly large body of students because of two conditions. One was that colleges, existing in large variety, cater to different needs, and good testing, counseling, and information services helped find for the majority of students the kind of college from which they could benefit. The other condition was the existence of an informal collegiate culture. This culture consisted of fraternities, clubs, and teams engaged in sports, debates, theater, journalism, and a great many other things. Membership in these groups often evoked great loyalty to and friendship within the group, great devotion to the purposes of the group, and intense competitiveness toward other groups. Achievement in these various group activities, such as sports, and in pursuit of the universal interests of youth, such as dating, counted in this culture more than scholarship. The values implicit in this culture were consistent with the beliefs and purposes of American society. Participation in these group activities was a good preparation for the combination of ruthless competitiveness and personal loyalty to one's team of coworkers that was so important in business. It also introduced young people effectively to the universalistic values of the non-kinship society of their peers, another important initiation for life in a socially and spatially mobile society in which one's team of coworkers changes from time to time. At the same time, the atmosphere was, so to speak, educational, since the activities did not carry over to adult life. They were, to some extent, also supervised by adults, and the sponsorship of these activities by the alumni established a bond between youth and adults. In this sheltered freedom of collegiate culture, young men and women could learn to know themselves. The activities were interesting and challenging. At the same time, they took place in a controlled environment and were regarded as play, so that one could go far in experimenting without running the risk of incurring lifelong liabilities. All this still did not amount to creating a firm purpose for the students in their studies. But it helped them, as it was so often said, "to find themselves."

Although it was crude and often corrupt, there were elements in this collegiate culture that represented some of the native values of the country. In the better colleges it helped students to learn that the rough and tumble of competitive life for which they prepared could be made consistent with democracy, altruism, and generosity.

In this manner college experience lent a broader moral meaning to the vocation of business, the way of life that many college students looked forward to. Having thus been helped by the college to establish an identity, students could also appreciate the intellectual and aesthetic purposes of the college. Their loyalty to the college, aroused perhaps by the nonintellectual aspects of college life, could make them appreciative and even receptive to science, scholarship, and art.

But this collegiate culture was never effectively integrated with academic studies. Academic achievement did not score highly in the scale of collegiate values, and academic teachers tended to keep aloof from this culture and often despised it as a falsification of the academic purposes of the college. Fraternities and sororities introduced into colleges snobbery and social discrimination that were inconsistent with the universalistic values of learning. The worst part of it was that college and alumni sponsorship of competitive sports, especially of football, often led to academic corruption, such as the awarding of scholarships to football players, and worse.

Furthermore, the effectiveness of this collegiate culture depended on a coherence between the college and its environment. There was careful nurturance of the relationship between the college and its alumni, of a feeling of responsibility for the college by the alumni, and of a degree of congruence between the values of the students, alumni, and the college. Consequently, collegiate culture was an effective educational influence in colleges that catered to a distinct class of students coming from college-educated families and preferably from the region of the college itself. Even in the most successful cases, however, there was a discrepancy between this informal education and the formal, intellectual part of the curriculum (Ben-David, 1972, pp. 78–81).[4]

PROBLEMS OF THE LIBERAL ARTS COLLEGE TODAY The conditions of college study changed during the 1950s and the 1960s, probably as a result of increased educational and other mobility and the spectacular shift of occupational prestige from business and politics to the professions, especially to the academic profession. An increasingly larger fraction of students came to consider college education as a preparation for a professional career, or a period when one could choose such a career, thus eliminating or at least considerably diminishing the problem of catering to the needs of the "general" student who wanted to obtain only a first-level degree. By 1961 three-fourths of college seniors intended to go to graduate school, and an increasing proportion of them actually did go (Davis, 1964, p. 11).

As a result, students who are not inclined to specialized study or to scholarship are likely to be impelled by college studies to enter some kind of graduate school. This is reminiscent of what has always been the situation in Europe and most other countries. Graduate education, unlike college, trains people for specific careers in each of which there is only a limited demand. But, as the European precedents show, demand for professional-administrative careers in public service can be increased artificially through political pressure. There are signs that something like this may be happening in the United States, as witnessed by the proliferation of regulatory and public service agencies congruent with the prevalence of antibusiness attitudes among students and with their occupational and political attitudes in general (Gallup, 1975).

Nonetheless, the attraction of a liberal arts program that enables students to orient themselves intellectually without holding back those who have chosen an educational goal is still great, and it has continued to prevail even in the junior colleges. And, in principle, the need for a general higher education at a time when about half of the 18-year-olds enter college is greater than ever. The problem is that, probably more than before, the ability of a large fraction of the students to benefit

[4] On the social functions of American youth culture—of which collegiate culture used to be the prototype—see Parsons (1949).

from high-level studies is limited. At the same time, the ability of the college community to absorb these students socially, and to give them a morally and aesthetically meaningful education, has greatly diminished. There is little moral consensus and less moral authority in the college, even in such matters as the definition of good taste, reasonable manners, and acceptable appearance.

But American colleges have had such problems before, and as long as they continue to have some educational and administrative independence, and financial incentive to search for a solution, they will find ways of dealing with them.

THE NEED FOR GENERAL EDUCATION IN EUROPE While these developments occurred in the United States, the systems of higher education in most other countries also grew rapidly. European countries now have higher education attendance rates of from 12 to 22 percent of the age group, and Canada and Japan have had rates even higher than that for many years (Organisation for Economic Co-operation and Development, 1974 *b*, pp. 24, 48). The United States, with its traditionally much higher rates of attendance, was to a large extent the model for this development. Those who advocated extension of higher education referred to the United States for evidence that such expansion was possible as well as economically and politically desirable and that only undue conservatism and restrictiveness prevented the expansion of the European systems. However, although the numerical strength of American higher education has been due mainly to the college, of both the liberal arts and the semiprofessional variety, this feature was not imitated in Europe or elsewhere. Only in Japan was general education during the first two years of university made compulsory, and this requirement was introduced by the American occupational authorities. There has been an attempt, since 1968, to make the first two years of university study into a formal general education program (with many electives) in France. But neither of these schemes has given rise to a sustained educational effort or an independent and respected liberal arts degree.[5]

[5]In France there is such a degree but it carries no prestige. In Japan the general education courses at the University of Tokyo, situated outside the main campus, actually became an independent university. Elsewhere in Japan or in other countries (except, of course, in the United States and to some extent in Britain) there is no degree in general education.

It is surprising that so much attention was paid to the American universities and hardly any to the liberal arts college. This was perhaps because of the changing and increasingly preparatory character of the American college. Therefore, the recent expansion of higher education in Europe only reinforced the old tendency of turning some fields into quasi-general education courses. This time these were the newly introduced social sciences, and in some places, notably in Germany, also the study of the national language and literature. Because these studies have often lacked reasonable academic standards (the social sciences expanded so rapidly that there just were not enough competent teachers), and because of the deeply ingrained politicization of the universities, the results in Europe have been much more directly political. Politics returned to the universities after a lull between the Second World War and the mid-1960s, when the booming economy absorbed with no difficulty the still relatively small numbers of graduates and when the postwar consensus about liberal democracy was still strong. As soon as university expansion overtook the growth of the economy, and the spirit of liberalism forged in the war dissipated, there reemerged on the Continent student activists who concentrated their interest on radical totalitarian politics, usually to the exclusion of serious scholarly study (although occasionally devoting considerable effort to the mastery of party dogma and tradition).

Of course, the political student revolts of the 1960s began in the United States.[6] These were triggered by specific events, namely, the campaign against racial discrimination and the Vietnam War. As these issues have been settled, the politicization of universities and colleges has considerably abated. This is not to say that the problem has been settled once and for all, or even until the next major societywide crisis. As has been seen, the ability of the college to provide moral guidance has been considerably weakened. But at least there is a serious attempt to provide a meaningful and useful education to all.

In Europe, especially on the continent, the situation is different. The disturbances erupted—in imitation of the American example—as a result of an accumulation of grievances against the ineffectiveness of university education and sustained agita-

---

[6] Violent student politics had been endemic in Japan a long time before. But there, too, disturbances became widespread and frequent only in the late 1960s.

tion and provocations by radical students. The resulting politicization of the university has been much longer lasting and far more pervasive than in the United States, or even in England. The reasons for this will be explored in some detail in Chapter 6, but it should be pointed out here that one of the reasons for the longer-lasting effects of politicization in Europe may be related to the traditional absence of any moral guidance by the universities, and of the lack of any attention to the problem of general education. Membership in totalitarian groups at these universities probably performs a function similar to that of the collegiate culture in the past in the United States (and England). It provides an environment in which young people in search of identity can find leaders to follow and can enter personal relationships and join groups that have a discipline to control the impulses of youth. These are particularly important for students who have no definite intellectual or vocational goal in their studies. Universities in continental Europe and Japan do not have the leadership, the organization, or even a serious incentive to remedy this situation. Many teachers feel no loyalty or even responsibility toward the institutions in which they work, since their civil service status, coupled with academic freedom, gives them a feeling of complete security and independence. These teachers are content to tolerate the politicization and even the corruption of certain universities or certain fields within universities (Domes & Frank, 1975). Since university government is based on the free cooperation of individual teachers, even a minority of teachers disloyal to the institution are capable of preventing the university from taking effective measures against disruption and corruption. Of course, governments have occasionally tried to counteract these tendencies, with limited success. But the reestablishment of reasonable standards of conduct and academic responsibility is in itself not enough to solve the problem of the increasing numbers of students who have little chance of entering professional careers of the kind for which they are trained and who go to the university in search of a meaningful identity and an education that helps to orient them toward a vocation.

MAINTAINING GENERAL EDUCATION In summary, it seems that general higher education as defined here—namely, as the education of the student who does not study for a specific career—is a growing educational need.

Catering to this need made possible the growth and democratization of higher education in the United States; and if other countries follow the American example, which they have done and probably will do in the future, they will have to adopt some kind of college education. In principle, there is the Soviet alternative of expanding higher semiprofessional education, but it is doubtful that such an alternative can work satisfactorily in a free society. In most semiprofessional fields it is difficult to build up an intellectually meaningful and interesting curriculum, and it is almost impossible to find teachers capable of teaching such subjects satisfactorily. And since the adaptability of students trained in such a framework is very limited, it can work only in an economy in which there is comprehensive and detailed planning and direction of manpower to specific jobs.

However, as has been seen, none of the existing systems of higher education would be capable of instituting programs of general higher education. Even if they were willing to institute such programs—which they have opposed until now on philosophical grounds—they would still lack the required internal organization. The likelihood that they would be prompted to develop programs at the urging or command of governments is small. Of course, governments that pay for higher education can force universities into such programs, as MacArthur's occupational authority did in Japan, but if the programs are contrived uniformly according to some central directive, they are bound to be ineffective. Since general education has to cater to the largest variety of students, it can be successful only if there are different programs and constant change and experimentation. At least this is what the cases surveyed here suggest. The only sustained and viable effort at academic general education—that in the United States—has been such a pluralistic enterprise. And standard general educational curricula have been difficult to maintain even on the secondary school level.

Only decentralization and the consideration of the particular needs of different student publics can ensure that the education of the "general" student—in contrast to one who prepares for a specific career—will not be overlooked. But it will not ensure the quality of this education. In fact, it may constitute a danger to educational standards, because educators will be under pressure to accept the educational notions of uneducated publics and to sanction unsatisfactory school performance by students.

Indeed the American college has often been under such pressures, and adjustment to it has been possible only through the not-quite-satisfactory mechanisms of the informal collegiate culture.

What ensured the maintenance and occasional improvement of standards in American higher education were the status hierarchy among institutions and competition for excellence in research. The elite institutions, such as the Ivy League colleges that catered to a public interested in high-quality education, served as a model and a challenge for the rest. Their prestige, as long as it was based on a measurable and generally valued quality, established a hierarchy based on educational standards. But with the decline of a recognized class hierarchy that sanctioned an educated style of life and the practice of an enlightened religiosity, the only scale of excellence that could claim general validity was research. This tended to shift the emphasis in college education toward preparation for graduate school and led to the abandonment of moral education by the colleges altogether. Therefore, the problem of finding a basis for an effective system of general education is closely tied to the function of research at the universities. We turn, therefore, to that question.

5. Research and Training for Research

As has been pointed out in the previous chapters, the idea that research had to be an important part of higher education was the distinguishing characteristic of the nineteenth-century German university. From there the idea spread to other countries, and by the end of the nineteenth century it was accepted practically everywhere.

Opponents of the research university were not lacking, from Cardinal Newman of Oxford to President Hutchins of Chicago (Hutchins, 1936, pp. 116–117). However, their opposition was not based on a critical analysis of the aims and achievements of the research university, but on a preference for an altogether different educational idea.

Recent critics of the research university have drawn attention to the more intrinsic problem of potential incompatibility between excellence in teaching, especially of undergraduates, and excellence in research. They have considered the problem in terms of a conflict of interests. Research takes time and requires the best efforts of the research worker. It may also require frequent travel. All these may—indeed are likely to—interfere with teaching, especially if the rewards of research are greater than those of teaching. And they invariably tend to be, because the fame of a good teacher rarely spreads beyond the local community, whereas the results of successful research are known all over the world (Kerr, 1963, pp. 64–65).

The problem, however, is not simply that research, instead of making teaching more interesting and more effective, may actually compete with it for the time and efforts of the teachers. The relationship between the two kinds of efforts is actually much more complicated than is usually assumed. To put it crudely, knowledge that can be taught no longer requires inves-

93

tigation, while knowledge that still needs to be investigated cannot yet be taught. Teaching may thus interfere with research, and vice versa, not only because they compete for time, but also because—in spite of their close relationship— they have different aims and require different approaches, different talents, and different facilities. Far from being a natural match, research and teaching can be organized within a single framework only under specific conditions. The purpose of this chapter is to explore those conditions and see how and to what extent they were realized in different countries.

Teaching requires a body of established authoritative knowledge, and none of the "progressive" methods of education has changed this basic fact. Traditional systems of higher education have been integrated bodies of knowledge, such as Confucian or scholastic philosophy, that could be taught as a whole. Later humanistic learning in Europe, which represented a greater variety of scholarly and literary traditions, disturbed but did not entirely destroy this unity. The learned person could still master all the "important" knowledge. Although this knowledge was not tied into a comprehensive philosophical system, it still had something like a unified structure. Mastery of classical languages was the key to all important learning, and the different parts of the cultural tradition were arranged in a relatively stable structure. Philosophical and literary classics (the latter were also treated partly as philosophy) were the center of all learning.[1] Theology, law, mathematics, medicine, and the natural sciences formed an increasingly remote periphery. Since the principal sources in all these fields were in Greek and Latin (with some in Arabic and Hebrew), knowledge depended on linguistic ability and correct philological interpretation.

In these relatively closed traditions of higher learning, combining research with teaching presented no difficulty since the difference between elementary and advanced knowledge was not one of substance or certainty, but one of mastery. Original

---

[1] See, for example, the description of the centrality of classics and mathematics at Oxford and Cambridge and the late recognition of other fields in the nineteenth century in Gillispie (1950), or the importance of Latin and of the study of ancient medical classics in the medical faculty in Paris in the eighteenth century in Taton (1964, pp. 179–181). For nineteenth-century France see Zeldin (1967, pp. 64–66), and for Germany, see Paulsen (1921, pp. 734–749).

research consisted of novel interpretation or systematization of the tradition and could be done as a part of the organization of the material for teaching. For academic teachers in the humanities the ideal of their being original investigators was not a nineteenth-century innovation. The university had been a seat of creative scholarship in philosophy throughout the Middle Ages, and many universities continued to employ original scholars throughout the seventeenth and eighteenth centuries (Irsay, 1935, pp. 13–23, 90–103; Sloan, 1971, pp. 23–32). Furthermore, the kind of teaching with which this research was, so to speak, naturally integrated was in general education, because interpretation and systematization of knowledge was always based on the general philosophical and philological tradition. If there was a tension between the different functions of higher education, it was between general education (philosophy and philology) and research on the one hand, and professional education on the other. This was only a potential tension, however, because the universities simply left practical training for the professions to apprenticeship and contented themselves with teaching the basic philological-philosophical traditions of the professions.

In contrast to the humanistic or earlier scholastic traditions, the experimental research that emerged in the natural sciences at the end of the seventeenth century was unsuitable to be linked with teaching. With the exception of certain parts of physics and astronomy, knowledge in the natural sciences consisted of observations of empirical phenomena interpreted in a more or less ad hoc manner and vague theories that carried little authority (Hahn, 1971, pp. 31–34). Indeed, only a few of the outstanding scientists of the end of the seventeenth and of the eighteenth century were teachers, and even those who were did not usually connect their teaching to their research. They worked in private laboratories and did not involve students in their work (McKie, 1952).[2] Therefore the backwardness of the instruction in the natural sciences at the eighteenth-century universities was not merely the result of the corruption from which these institutions suffered at that time; these fields were simply inferior to the humanities as educational subjects. They

---

[2] Leiden, Göttingen, and the Scottish universities were to some extent exceptions, since they tried to cultivate natural sciences. But these sciences were still peripheral to the humanistic studies even in these progressive universities.

were more like arts and crafts, which explains why the eighteenth-century reformers wanted specialized, scientific professional-training institutions.

It was realized that the establishment of such specialized institutions would not eliminate the growing disjunction between the still-scholastic, humanistic general education and the scientific-technical professional education. Therefore, philosophers groped for a new integration of learning based on contemporary scientific and philosophical culture. Later in the eighteenth century, particularly in Germany, their reform also included the study of vernacular literatures and of the histories of European nations. These ideas of reform did not envisage turning the university into a conglomeration of research institutes, but were based on the assumption that the classical tradition could be replaced with new fields of study that had some internal coherence and that could be taught through books and lectures. No one envisaged breaking higher education into disconnected disciplinary studies topped by specialized research of specific problems by advanced students (König, 1970, pp. 154–160; Schnabel, 1959, vol. 1, pp. 453–457).

FIRST ATTEMPTS AT INTEGRATING RESEARCH AND TEACHING IN FRANCE The contents of the studies and the way their coherence was to be established were different from system to system. The dominant view in France was the encyclopedist idea of a comprehensive study of man, society, and nature, based principally on the study of the natural and social ("moral") sciences and interpreted in a framework of a kind of positivistic philosophy (Baker, 1975, pp. 47–55, 285–303). In Germany the philosophical synthesis was based mainly on the traditions of literary and historical scholarship and allowed only a negligible role for the new natural sciences (Schnabel, vol. 1, 1959, pp. 453–457).

The French experiment was discontinued in the later Napoleonic period. It is difficult to decide whether this failure was due to political conditions or whether the encyclopedist program was unrealizable. But even that scheme, in which natural sciences played a central role, incorporated no clear plans for actually linking research in experimental science to teaching. The link was indirect and was to consist only of subjecting the system of education to the guidance of leading scientists who themselves did not necessarily teach (Crosland, 1967, pp. 223–231; Liard, 1888, pp. 266–275). Outstanding scientists were often employed as teachers, not because teaching was connected in any important way with research, but because they needed a source of income that allowed them enough time to do their research privately. High administrative or political appointments (for example, a seat in Napoleon's senate) served this purpose equally well, but, of course, such positions were scarce.

Thus, this first attempt to link higher education—and education in general—to science avoided the difficulty inherent in linking education (which is essentially the transmission of a tradition) with research (the transformation of tradition) by trying to distill into teaching that part of the scientific tradition which could be considered more or less self-contained and by allowing research to be pursued separately. In practice, science in French education meant mainly mathematics and the theoretical aspects of physics, while the place allotted to experimental science was very limited. This approach was maintained under the Napoleonic retrenchment of the reforms.

UNITY OF RESEARCH AND TEACHING IN GERMANY   The original German idea of the unity of research and teaching was not so different from the French one. Research was conceived as work done in privacy and freedom (in *Einsamkeit und Freiheit*), while teaching was naturally public. In a way, the German system tried to assure through the formal organization of the university what French scientists were given informally, namely, a good income to make possible private research. If there was in Germany more desire to link the two activities, this was largely because of an emphasis on the study of humanities and philosophy rather than on the natural sciences as in the pre-Napoleonic reforms in France. Thus the unity of teaching and research could be conceived as scholars expounding the authoritative traditions of their field and introducing their original contributions to that tradition, illuminating it by asking new questions or organizing it in a new way. This was, of course, the old ideal of the teacher-scholar capable of interpreting the traditional body of learning in an original manner. It was modified only to the extent that knowledge was no longer regarded as consisting essentially of a single field. Even this statement has to be qualified, since the schools of idealistic philosophy that dominated Prussian universities still considered their systems the center around which all knowledge could be logically organized. But this claim was rejected by the majority of scholars in the empirical sciences, which meant mainly the philological fields (history, language, and literature). The experimental sciences were at that point only a peripheral part of university study, the bulk of which consisted, besides law and medicine, of historical and linguistic fields (Schnabel, vol. 3, 1959, pp. 3–128, 198–238).

Initially the results of this reform were similar to those of the French one with respect to the natural sciences. The German universities also tended to neglect experimental science, and some of them even attempted to propagate a philosophical, speculative approach to natural science, adopting the romantic *Naturphilosophie*. But because professors at the German universities were not limited by curricula approved by the ministries of education, they could introduce into their courses the topics of their specialized research.

Research in the technical sense of finding and exploring new problems in experimental science, or in field research in such areas as natural history or the budding social sciences, became part of the idea of the unity of teaching and research only later as a by-product of the initiatives taken by individual teachers to provide effective practical training to students intending to go into the professions. Originally, the seminars in the humanities were—as their name implies—intensive courses for future *Gymnasium* teachers, especially in the classical languages; laboratory instruction in the natural sciences began as an attempt to provide practical training for pharmacy students. In both of these instances students obtained a technical training that taught them the tools and procedures employed in research. They were not taught this in the expectation of their becoming research workers, but they needed it for their work as teachers or pharmacists (Gustin, 1975; Paulsen, 1921, pp. 258–259).

Laboratory research of teachers and students, now the pinnacle of higher education, had its humble beginnings in the 1820s in what were considered trade courses for pharmacists not quite befitting a university and which, therefore, were initially conducted as a private affair of the teachers. This is how the laboratory of Justus Liebig, which became the model for all university laboratories in chemistry, started at Giessen. Such courses had existed before the universities were reformed, but their functions changed subsequent to the reforms because of the concatenation of several circumstances. One was the rise of an academic market for teachers. This compelled the ministries of education of the German states, which administered the universities, to compete with each other for academic reputation. Such reputation could be gained mainly through having famous scientists on the staff. Therefore, the universities developed the natural sciences and supported laboratory research, as the scientists demanded (Zloczower, 1966). The second circumstance was that to some extent this was an exceptional age in the development of learning. Chemistry, physics, and physiology made tremendous strides in the late eighteenth and early nineteenth centuries. All of a sudden they became well-organized bodies of significant knowledge that were sufficiently delimited to be taught by a (single) teacher. At the same time, the philological study of historical and literary sources, inspired by the scientific spirit, also became more interpretive and systematic. The aim of these studies was now not only correct textual interpretation, but explanation of the internal logic or rules of language and literary forms, and of causal relationships in history. What had been until then nonphilosophical traditions of such artisans as "chemists," and schoolmasters teaching Latin and Greek, became logically related to the higher reaches of philosophic (in today's parlance, scientific) thought. All this benefited teaching immensely. It was possible to present the subject matter in an interesting and theoretically coherent way, yet so that the theory was still directly relevant to the art of the pharmacist, the schoolmaster, or (in physiology) the medical doctor.

As a result, it was possible to teach and train pharmacists, physicians, and high school (*Gymnasium* or *lycée*) teachers in the theory and practice of their arts, and at the same time inspire the abler students to do research and to encourage them to eventually enter academic careers. There was no need to provide much further instruction to the research student. The newly systematized disciplines contained all the theory there was to know, and the technical skills useful to the professional practitioners (doctors, pharmacists) were sufficient also for the research worker. In practice, the integration of theory and research meant that pharmacists, physicians, and high school teachers could be taught together with future research workers to the benefit of all.

This transformed the integration of research with teaching, as well as the relationship between research and general education on the one hand, and training for the professions on the other. Research ceased to be conducted in privacy, but began to be carried on in the community of teachers and students. The former directed the work of the students and actually organized it in a way that extended their own research and provided practical apprenticeship to the students as a preparation for both professional practice and research.

The philosophical rationalization of the new practice was different in the humanities and in the natural sciences. Teachers in the humanities denied that their purpose now included training future *Gymnasium* teachers, for they believed this would compromise the pure-research orientation of the universities. Those in chemistry and the natural sciences in general tended to adopt a utilitarian philosophy stressing the practical usefulness of research for industrial and other applications (Gustin, 1975; Paulsen, 1921, pp. 258–259, 274–275). But the practices behind these apparently opposing philosophies were identical. The teachers taught their fields on an advanced level, based on up-to-date research, and taught the techniques as tools of research. They did not teach how to apply these techniques to manufacturing better shoe polish at a lower cost, or to teaching Greek or Latin grammar to high school students more effectively or to a larger number of students in fewer hours. Since, however, one had to master research techniques to succeed in these more mundane pursuits, university research training in the humanities served those who wanted to engage in these professions as *Gymnasium* teachers just as training in chemistry and physiology served industrial chemists or medical doctors. The only difference was that the humanities denied any intention of serving practical purposes, while the natural sciences stressed the usefulness of research for practical purposes—positions, of course, that were not mutually exclusive.

In both cases, research now moved much closer to professional training than to general education. It was integrated with the former but sharply distinct from the latter. If any connection remained between research and the general educational ideal, it was merely philosophical, resting on the assertion that only through original research, no matter in what field, could one have the "experience" of a higher education.

EMERGING
DIFFICULTIES IN
THE
INTEGRATION
OF RESEARCH
AND TEACHING Evidently this period could not last long. Even in the very beginning there were fields of professional study that did not lend themselves to such unification. In engineering, for example, there was no way to teach the practical aspects of the field in close relation to a given theory, as was possible in pharmacy. The relationship between research and professional training was to a large extent fictitious in law and medicine as well, requiring a separation of teaching and training in clinical medicine and law practice from the study of the so-called basic disciplines in these fields. Indeed, French schools of engineering and medicine, which up until about 1840 were considered the most progressive in the world, made no attempts to integrate research with teaching.

But even in fields in which the integration worked well in the beginning, it broke down after a while as a result of two circumstances. Although, as has been seen, the universities did not regard research workers as professionals requiring a distinct training and career, but as an elite emerging from those who studied for (high school) teaching and the learned professions, the growth of higher education turned the academic teacher-researchers into members of something like a profession. To become an academic teacher one had to do original research, and the direction of research was determined by the opportunities to discover something new. These opportunities soon led to the rise of new specialties that could not be integrated with the needs of any practical profession or any high school teaching discipline. For example, philological research originating in the study of classics was extended to the study of European languages, history, and literature, only some of which were disciplines taught in high schools. Continued advancement required comparative studies, abstract linguistics, and sociology, all of which were unrelated to high school teaching or any "practical" profession. In these fields research was the only profession one could study for. There were similar developments in the natural sciences.

Of course, there was no theoretical difficulty in integrating teaching with research in these fields. But establishing such fields as disciplines in the universities implied a change in the purpose of the university and turned the idea of integration into a tautology; these fields were not studied except by people interested in research. And when they were taught as auxiliary courses for students preparing for careers other than research, such as medicine, then teaching them on a level reflecting, and linked to, up-to-date research did present a problem, and quite a serious one.

But the most important reason for the breakdown of the original idea of the integration of teaching and research was the basic discrepancy, noted in the beginning of this chapter, between disciplines that could be taught, and research. The idea that research takes place within a theoretically organized, teachable body of knowledge, so that theory guides research, which then corrects or fills in the gaps of theory, is an ideal state rarely approximated in reality. Soon after the natural science disciplines had been established at the universities there emerged types of research that did not fit into any disciplinary framework. Some of these, such as bacteriology, had practical success with obvious theoretical implications. But since the nature of those implications was still far from clear, the field did not have the structure expected from a recognized teaching discipline. For example, the chemical explanation of the vital process of fermentation challenged many scientists. But to engage in the investigation of such a question put one beyond the pale of systematic tradition in both chemistry and biology (Kohler, 1971; Zloczower, 1966).

Thus the transfer of the seat of research to the universities and its connection with teaching did not prevent a recurrence of the kind of research that could not be taught because it was not much more than organized groping in the dark or a search for a new structure in the no-man's-land between disciplinary boundaries. The knowledge required for such research usually included several disciplinary traditions, or rather parts of such traditions, but those traditions were not theoretically integrated. Therefore, the field could not be taught, and one could only learn about it through research apprenticeship.

In other cases, especially in physics, new fields arose that were just too highly specialized to be taught to anyone who was not preparing to become a research worker in one of them.[3] Laboratory instruction in physics at the universities lagged

[3] See Klein (1904, especially pp. 251–253). Starting from 1870, development in physical research was extremely rapid, and was greatly stimulated by industrial interests in electricity, telephone, telegraphy, and so on. See also Kundt (1893). Both authors stress the increasing specialization in physics.

behind such instruction in chemistry and physiology and began in earnest only in the 1860s. By the end of the century physics became the intellectually most interesting branch of experimental science. But unlike chemistry and physiology, advanced physics research was of little use in the training for any profession except that of a research physicist. And even this statement has to be qualified, because specializations in physics very soon became so technical that one could not speak of a research physicist in general, but only of one in a certain branch of the discipline. To make things worse, research in experimental physics was very expensive and required semi-industrial facilities difficult for the university to accommodate. This was when the term *big science (Grosswissenschaft)* was coined to describe the state of physics (Busch, 1959, pp. 73–75, 81–82).

Therefore, the integration of research and teaching, which had been the main source of strength of German science throughout the middle of the nineteenth century, became a problem for the German system by the turn of the century. As a result, teaching was institutionally separated from research, first within the university through the concentration of research in "institutes" that were personal research establishments of professors virtually separated from the university, and subsequently—in 1911, through the founding of the *Kaiser Wilhelm Gesellschaft*—by establishing pure research institutions without any teaching functions at all. But these were solutions designed for specific instances. The leading position of the university, as well as its principle of the unity of teaching and research, was maintained, and care was taken to avoid competition between the new institutes and the universities. Thus there was no solution to the problems involved in the integration of increasingly specialized research with the training of professionals requiring much less specialization.

IMPLANTATION AND TRANSFORMA-TION OF THE GERMAN MODEL IN BRITAIN A similar situation developed in Britain, but there the problem never became as acute as in Germany. Since the eighteenth century, England has followed the initiatives in research organization made in other countries, rather than initiating her own changes. Furthermore, English research has relied mainly on private support. Thus it could develop fields of research that looked promising without being hampered very much by the inertia of its own official institutions. The English universities did no scientific research and practically no science teaching until the middle of the nineteenth century (although the Scottish universities did). At that time they began imitating the German model to the extent of accepting the principle that academic teachers had to be active in research.

But the universities were private institutions (as late as 1938–39 only 35.8 percent of their budget came from the central government) with widely different financial resources (Halsey & Trow, 1971, p. 63). As a result, the adoption of the principle that university teaching had to be integrated with research did not give rise to a standard practice followed by all institutions, or even by all the departments within the same institution. It was taken for granted that Oxford and Cambridge had the highest standards, followed at close range by different parts of the London complex of colleges and schools—the so-called University of London—and then by the other universities. The Scottish universities constituted a separate tradition and had their own standards.

All the universities considered their foremost task the effective training of students for their intended careers. In the provincial universities, this meant training for the old and new "learned" professions. Oxford and Cambridge were somewhat freer in this respect, since many of their students considered themselves part of an intellectual elite that could choose careers in politics, civil service, or academic teaching. Since their future was secure, they could choose their fields of study freely according to their intellectual inclinations and explore the limits and the style of their intellectual ability by trying to master whatever seemed to be challenging.

Students at Oxford or Cambridge were relatively few and highly qualified, and the teacher-student ratio was much higher than in Germany, so that students were given a great deal of individual attention as well as freedom (Flexner, 1930, pp. 274–287). This made it possible for students to spend relatively less time on the acquisition of the codified parts of the disciplines, and for teachers to introduce some specialized work even at the first-degree level. But it has to be emphasized that this was done satisfactorily only at the two elite universities and in a few select departments of the other institutions. The rest of the system placed much more emphasis on straightforward teaching and professional training than on research, and few students ever became professional research workers (Truscot, 1943). Furthermore, even in the elite schools there was a great deal of straightforward teaching by tutors and lecturers, many of whom were not active in research.

A further characteristic that made the integration of research with teaching in Britain different from that in the German system was the departmental structure. Although its origins lay in the revulsion of the dons at Oxford and Cambridge from German-style professional authority (an attitude stemming from prescientific conservative tradition) (Halsey & Trow, 1971, pp. 147–148), the departmental structure also suited the postdisciplinary stage of scientific research of the late nineteenth century far better than the German chair system. Since at this stage no single person could master an entire field, and since research was often only loosely related to the core disciplinary tradition, a group of teachers, each working in a different part of the field, could give a more realistic picture of the state of the art than teaching dominated by a single person obliged to create the semblance of a coherent system where there was none.

While the British system adopted the German principle of integration of research and teaching with reasonable success, it was never committed, to the extent that the German system was, to see in the universities the main seat of advanced fundamental research. It was taken for granted that there were fields of research, including some kinds of fundamental research, that could not be reconciled with the educational functions of the universities. It was accepted that this type of research should be supported by the government to the extent that its results were expected to contribute to knowledge in a field of important social concern. So-called research councils were organized in medicine, agriculture, and subsequently in several other fields that created their own establishments and also allocated funds for research at the universities. Eventually research councils were also established to finance university research in nonapplied fields (Science Research Council, 1965; Social Science Research Council, 1965), but this occurred under American influence (Albu, 1975). In any event, the relatively smooth integration of research with teaching at the leading British universities was the result of the flexible way in which the principle was adopted. In many parts of the system there was

little research and much more teaching and professional training, and much research was done outside the universities.
Integration of the two activities was always subordinated to
training the students. Therefore, apart from some fields of
natural science in which there was a demand for professionals
trained in research techniques, integration of research and
teaching was successful mainly at the elite universities. In
those, many able students planned to enter research as a profession, and a high proportion of the others were intellectually
equipped and motivated to acquire some competence in
research.

IMPACT OF THE GERMAN MODEL IN FRANCE The Western European country that was influenced last and
least by the German model was France. That country had a long
tradition of government support for a few selected research
workers and a higher education reform that did not involve
integration of teaching and research. Only when German
advances made it evident that informal scientific training and
personal support of research was obsolete was an attempt made
to develop research within the framework of French higher
education. However, this did not lead to the adoption of the
principle of unity of teaching and research. Teaching for the
different academic degrees and examinations remained
unchanged, and many appointments in higher education went
to people not outstanding in research. But in recognition of the
fact that research itself was now on the way to becoming a
profession, a new institution was created in 1868, the so-called
Ecole pratique des hautes études. This initially was not a separate
school but an organization to support and develop certain units
in the different schools and faculties to a level where they could
give training in research to those interested in it. Beyond this
no general attempt was made to link teaching and study to
research, although there was an increasing preference to
appoint as professors people with attainment in research and to
encourage research at universities. But the organization that
finances most of the basic research in France, the *Centre national
de la recherche scientifique* (established in 1939), is still a distinct
organization that has facilities of its own and that has no
concern with teaching. This selective support of research in
certain parts of higher education has remained characteristic of
the French system.

Thus, in spite of the fundamental differences in the structure of higher education in France and in Britain, the two systems integrated research into the institutions of higher education in similar ways. In both countries research was to be found only in parts of the system, although these parts were selected differently in the two countries. A further similarity between France and Britain was that neither assumed that all pure research had to take place in institutions of higher education. In France, as in Britain, nonuniversity research institutions played an important role in research. However, in Britain, research was in principle integrated with teaching, whereas in France the principle of the unity of research and teaching was adopted only in 1968, and it is not yet clear to what extent this is taken seriously. Furthermore, in Britain integration was carried out most consistently in the top universities, which set a standard for the system as a whole. In France the task of financing and—to a large extent—of organizing research has always been entrusted to separate organizations (*Ecole pratique des hautes études; Centre national de la recherche scientifique*). As a result, there is an institutional separation between higher educational and research policy (Organisation for Economic Co-operation and Development, 1966, p. 41). Thus, once introduced, research at the British universities spread as a result of the internal mechanism of the system, while in France it had to be periodically reinforced by new institutions and centrally initiated reforms.

UNITY OF RESEARCH AND TEACHING: IDEA AND REALITY AT THE TURN OF THE CENTURY

Viewing the situation in the three leading European countries at the end of the nineteenth century, one is struck by the lag between the ideas about universities and reality. This was when the idea of the unity of teaching and research was almost universally accepted in academic circles (it was also widely acclaimed in France, even though the inertia of the system prevented its official adoption). Yet it was obvious that the implementation of the ideal posed serious problems. Research became increasingly specialized, and much of it was unconnected with professional practice. This was particularly true in physics, the most interesting and most rapidly developing branch of experimental science of that period. It was not possible any longer to train research workers and to do advanced research as a by-product of professional training or to train professionals as a by-product of teaching and doing basic research (as required by the German academic ideology). Direct decisions had to be made about the scale of support of basic research and training for basic research as a distinct activity, and these were difficult because there was no discernible specific demand for basic research.

NEW PATTERNS OF INTEGRATION IN THE UNITED STATES This problem was, if not solved, at least temporarily averted by the emergence of the American graduate school as a separate level of training students for advanced professional work, including research as a profession. As has been pointed out, this innovation was considered by its originators an imitation of the German model and an adoption of the German philosophy about the relationship between research and teaching. But only the contents of graduate studies followed the German model, although in a greatly improved way. The separation of graduate from undergraduate education, implying the integration of research with the former but not with the latter, was in effect carrying further the logic implied in the British and the French tradition, according to which only some, but not all, higher teaching had to be integrated with research. However, the definition of the part of higher education to become so integrated became much sharper in the United States than in those two European countries. It was not the institutions designed to educate the country's elite, or isolated units of self-selected masters and disciples, that were to be engaged in research, but a specially organized part of the university attended by graduates with formal educational qualifications, who would study to enter professional research careers, such as academic teaching, or other types of professional work in which research was a necessary or useful component. Research was conceived of here as regular professional work for which one was trained, and not as an elite activity for which one was somehow "chosen" through individual charisma.

This step eliminated the principal barriers to the development of this stage of "postdisciplinary" research. The fact that learning a specialty could lead only to research and not to the careers that most college graduates intended to enter was no longer a reason for its exclusion from the regular curriculum, because research was the principal career for which graduate schools trained their students. Training in fields that straddled several disciplines was more of a problem, because of the difficulties in devising a curriculum. But this was a technical problem rather than a philosophical or structural one.

Whether a specialty was adopted by universities or not did not primarily depend on its having a coherent intellectual tradition. If there was a demand for professional researchers or practitioners in the field, the specialty was adopted. Research and teaching in bacteriology, physical chemistry, education, business management, and clinical research in medicine were developed at American universities much more rapidly than in Europe.[4] In all these cases the core around which study and research are integrated is the solution or treatment of a problem requiring various combinations of disciplinary knowledge and technical skills. To the extent that the problem is well defined and the person to be trained is actually working on it in an advanced research project, or in clinical or other practical work, that person can integrate the otherwise disparate studies for himself or herself.

This new kind of advanced training in research prompted drastic changes in organization. Since every graduate department was actually a professional school, its organization came to resemble that of such schools. Professors were not appointed to represent the core of a discipline, but to represent as far as possible the whole range of specialties relevant to research in the field. The attitude toward complex instrumentation and facilities within university departments also changed. The apprehension that such facilities would introduce bureaucratic elements alien to the free spirit of the university was counterbalanced by the need to provide apprenticeship training for students. Such facilities were thought to be as necessary for graduate schools of arts and sciences as a teaching hospital would be for a medical school (Ben-David, 1972, pp. 95–101).

Because of these developments the university, at least in the United States, could continue to play a central role in advanced research, including research that required organization and relatively large-scale facilities. Furthermore, the university's role made it possible to avoid the intractable problem—which loomed large in Europe—of how and on what basis to support pure research. Instead of having to decide how much should be

[4]See Flexner (1925, pp. 223–226, and 1930, pp. 100–102, 162–172) for a highly critical view of some of these developments.

spent on research, or how the funds should be divided between different kinds of research, on the basis of some intrinsic criteria, it was possible to rely on some kind of market mechanism. Of course, before the Second World War the universities were not financed by the federal government, and so they could make individual decisions and compete with each other for research workers and funds obtained mainly from private foundations. But there was an additional market mechanism. Students decided in what fields to obtain higher degrees on the basis of demand for professional services, including research (Blank & Stigler, 1957; Freeman, 1971). Of course, outside demand for researchers was less than, for example, the demand for doctors or engineers. The principal field of employment for arts and sciences graduates was the academic system itself, so that in a way the decision to train students was a decision also to employ them, and vice versa.

But not entirely. The academic system consisted of several layers of institutions, and only a small fraction engaged in research and in training for research. As recently as 1948–49, 20 institutions granted nearly 70 percent of all the doctoral degrees in the United States (see Table 1).[5] Thus the market for Ph.D.'s went into primarily teaching institutions. Furthermore, all the elite departments also trained students for the master's degree in the same framework as they trained their doctoral candi-

[5]There has been also a decrease of concentration in Great Britain, but less than one would expect in view of the growth in the number of institutions (see Table 2).

TABLE 1 *Cumulative proportions of all doctorates conferred by the 5th, 10th, 15th, and 20th highest doctorate-conferring institutions in the United States, 1948–49 through 1970–71*

Number of institutions	1948–49	1957–58	1967–68	1970–71
5	.295	.223	.136	.125
10	.455	.366	.242	.222
15	.588	.472	.334	.303
20	.685	.553	.407	.370
	N = 5,293	N = 8,942	N = 23,091	N = 32,113
Total number of institutions	1,259	1,365	1,567	1,644

SOURCES: U.S. Office of Education (1949, 1959, 1969, 1973).

TABLE 2 Cumulative proportions of all doctorates conferred by the 3rd, 6th, and 9th highest doctorate-conferring institutions in Great Britain, 1934–35 through 1971–72

Number of institutions	1934–35	1949–50	1959–60	1971–72
3	.517	.581	.474	.265
6	.712	.740	.642	.427
9	.816	.846	.772	.529
	N = 673	N = 1,428	N = 2,004	
Total number of institutions	28	30	32	53

SOURCES: *Commonwealth Universities Yearbook* (various titles; 1936, 1952, 1962, 1973, 1974).

dates. Therefore, training for research was still part of a broader training for advanced professional work in general. The graduate school did not pursue pure knowledge for its own sake and induce young people to take up this pursuit without regard to the environment. The pursuit of pure knowledge was, of course, an ideal that many teachers and students believed in as well as practiced. But they—or if not they, the university administrators—were perfectly aware that in a democratic society the realization of this ideal depended in the long run on the extent to which this ideal was shared and on evidence that even those who did not share the ideal would eventually benefit from the knowledge produced by research.

The most tangible way of sharing the ideal with a much larger public was through college education. As has been pointed out, the reform and the spread of college education (and the rise of research in the chemical and electrical industries) were as much conditions of the success of the American graduate schools until the 1940s as the reform and the growth of *Gymnasium* education (and of the pharmaceutical and chemical industries) had been a condition of the rise of research in the German universities in the second and third quarters of the nineteenth century. But the scope offered by the college was much broader, and above all much more flexible, than that provided by the German *Gymnasium*. The elective principle of the college allowed the employment of teachers in a broad and changing variety of fields and specialties. And the greater maturity of the students and the academic freedom of the college prevented authorities from imposing on college teaching a straitjacket of prescribed disciplinary contents as was imposed in the German *Gymnasium*.

Another condition that probably aided the professionalization of research training in the United States was the much larger size of the market for trained researchers; its demand for relatively esoteric specialties was recognizable and relatively stable.

Finally, foundations that supported research without regard for either potential demand or for practical application, but simply for the sake of the advancement of knowledge, were still not required to make far-reaching decisions on the scientific merit of the fields involved or on such questions as how much the development of the field was worth. Until the 1930s, foundations usually supported fields of research in which the United States was still backward compared to the best work done elsewhere, so that both the fields themselves and the resources needed to attain an adequate level of research in them were known.[6]

Essentially, therefore, the American graduate schools operated within a framework of a market for professional research workers. They were primarily institutions for training researchers, and not research institutes in pure or applied science. Funds obtained for research unconnected with teaching were, until World War II, a small part of the university budget. Universities had few opportunities to develop research institutes in the universities that did not have to train graduate students as well, and they did not usually seek such opportunities.

For individual academic persons this framework allowed great freedom. They could engage in practically any kind of research, including research in new specialties or in interdisciplinary problems, and they could choose problems purely on the basis of intellectual interest. If such work was recognized as important and was followed by other research workers, research students would probably be interested in being trained in the field. Therefore, universities were often sympathetic to pure research enterprise by their teachers, even though they considered teaching and professional training their main functions. But it was not important to the university that individual teachers share the institutional scale of preference. The

[6]See, for example, Coben (1971).

universities could employ professors who were primarily research workers not much interested in teaching, because such professors would still attract and train graduate students. This type of professor would have conceived of the university as a research institute in everything but name, although this was actually not the case.

Thus the unity of teaching and research in this system underwent a drastic transformation. As in Britain, only the elite universities practiced the idea. But there was a differentiation in the United States system that did not exist elsewhere. Research and advanced training for research were by and large restricted to graduate departments with Ph.D. programs. These were only partially integrated with the training for professional practice other than research (in departments combining terminal master's degrees with doctoral programs, for example). Otherwise, the integration was indirect in the sense that teachers at professional schools (including those in terminal master's programs in the arts and sciences, and in education) tended to be Ph.D.'s who did some research with the participation of some of their students.

Another, probably even more important, difference between the American and the European situation was in the relationship between research and general education. Since general education hardly existed in Europe, it could not be integrated with research. But in the United States these two functions were integrated, at least to some extent. Professors at the best colleges were Ph.D.'s and those at the best universities also taught undergraduates. This created a great incentive to translate into the college curriculum increasing parts of the new knowledge created by research. This was an economic necessity, because—as has been pointed out—until the Second World War college teaching was the principal market for Ph.D.'s, and the economic health of most of the universities depended on enrollments. The importance of the effort to teach the results of research was that it lent some concrete operational meaning to the demand for pure research. Liberal education was an item of cultural comsumption separate from professional training. To the extent that there was a widespread demand for such education, and to the extent that this education was integrated with pure research as described here, one could speak of a measurable social demand for pure research.

CHANGES IN UNIVERSITY RESEARCH SINCE WORLD WAR II

Dramatic changes occurred in the uses of scientific research during the Second World War. At this time the immense research capacity of the graduate schools was harnessed to several research and development projects—including the largest in history, the development of the atomic bomb (Bush, 1946; Baxter, 1946/1968). Research expenditures rose precipitously, and so did the budgets of higher education (Table 3).

Research institutes of unprecedented size, such as the Lawrence Radiation Laboratory at Berkeley, and Argonne at Chicago, were set up in the universities and administered by them, although they were never really absorbed in the universities. All these events transformed the atmosphere and the horizon of the academics and, more significantly, of the university administrators. Research that was not necessarily related to teaching became a recognized function of the university, and it appeared that it would eventually become a major function (Kerr, 1963, pp. 42–43).

That the universities assumed this new function was almost inevitable. By the end of the war there was a community of highly competent professional research workers with high morale and outstanding leadership, and the universities would have been irresponsible to waste this capacity by cutting down research to the prewar level. The universities demanded that the federal government bear the financial responsibility for these extended research activities on the grounds that the gov-

TABLE 3
Expenditure on higher education and on research and development, compared with GNP, United States, 1920–1970 (dollar amounts in billions)

		Expenditure on higher education		Expenditure on research and development	
Year	*GNP*	*Dollars*	*Percentage of GNP*	*Dollars*	*Percentage of GNP*
1920	88.9	0.216	.24		
1930	90.4	0.632	.70		
1940	99.7	0.759	.76	0.340	.34
1950	284.8	2.662	.94	2.800	.98
1955	398.0			6.279	1.58
1960	503.7	6.617	1.31	13.730	2.73
1965	684.9	15.200	2.22	20.439	2.98
1970	974.1	24.900	2.56	26.000	2.66

SOURCES: U.S. Bureau of the Census (1957, p. 122; 1967, p. 109; 1972, pp. 106, 312–313, 521); Organisation for Economic Co-operation and Development (1968, p. 30).

ernment was responsible for getting the universities into large-scale research work and that research was a public good.[7]

But it was evident that government funding presented a problem for the universities. No one in the universities or in government wanted to preserve the wartime arrangements of having specific missions determined by the federal government, because none of the parties was interested in direct control of research and because there were no missions such as there had been during the war.

The problem, as seen by those who designed the new mechanisms of research support, was to maintain federal funding of research on a high level while returning the task of performing the research and organizing adequate facilities for it to the universities (in effect to the graduate schools of the leading universities). By this means they hoped to preserve freedom and flexibility without forgoing the advantages of direct and stable support.[8] The outcome has been a complicated system that includes both governmental research institutes, agencies granting funds for projects, and various types of contract research. But the main performer of basic research remains the university.[9]

The main features of the system emerged only in the late 1950s. Until then, partly because of relatively slow expansion of support and partly because of concepts inherited from the 1930s, efforts were made to justify research within the frame-

---

[7] Bush (1945) is the main document on the relationship of the federal government to science that developed after the war.

[8] Of the gross national expenditure on research and development (GERD) in the United States in 1963–64, 63.8 percent came from government funds, but only 18.1 percent of it was spent on work performed by government institutions. Universities were allotted about 13 percent of the GERD, about half of which came from the government (see Organisation for Economic Co-operation and Development, 1967a, pp. 60, 64). The corresponding percentages for 1973 were 53,15.5, and 9.4 (National Science Foundation, 1976, pp. 173, 174).

[9] About half the funds for basic research in 1963–64 went to universities. The rest was divided between industry (25 percent), government (16 percent), and private, nonprofit research institutes (9 percent) (Organisation for Economic Co-operation and Development, 1967a, p. 59). In 1973 the share of the universities went up to 62 percent, and industry, government, and private, nonprofit institutes were down to 16, 15, and 7 percent, respectively. The budget spent on basic research in federally funded research and development centers administered by the universities amounted to 20 percent of the basic research budgets of the universities proper in 1963 and to 14 percent in 1973 (National Science Foundation, 1976, p. 186).

work of the professional training functions of the university. There was considerable effort to demonstrate the practical uses of research and its importance in training for the professions.

Perhaps the rise of professionalism in the late 1940s and early 1950s resulted from this situation. Publicly supported service industries such as medicine, agriculture, economic and social planning and policy, and personal counseling services (psychiatry, clinical psychology, social work, etc.) seemed to be the most promising fields for research enterprise. These fields of public concern enjoyed a tradition of public support for research because there was a good prospect that their research could eventually be linked to the training of practicing professionals.

There was also support for basic research in nonapplied fields through the National Science Foundation. But it was taken for granted that this type of support would be limited and that the bulk of the national expenditure on research would go to purposes connected with practical applications.

This situation changed after the rise into space of the first Soviet *Sputnik*, a scientific-technological achievement of military significance in which the Soviet Union surpassed the United States. The event resurrected the motive of catching up with other countries. But the methods of this "catching up" and the context in which it occurred were very different from prewar antecedents. In the 1920s and 1930s, catching up with other countries (mainly Germany) meant introducing new fields, or subfields, of research. This was done by the universities, who were aided by private foundations, and the intended direct beneficiary was American science and graduate education. Thus the foreign model actually set standards and levels of support of research. But in the 1950s, following *Sputnik*, American universities could learn very little from their Soviet counterparts. In spite of *Sputnik*, American science was not backward compared to Soviet science. It was argued, perhaps with some justification, that American science education, from grade school through college, was in some ways deficient in comparison with the Soviet effort and, of course, American backwardness in rocket and space technology was obvious. Progress in science education required increased investment of resources in teaching; progress in the technology required a new effort in mission-oriented research, like those efforts that led to the development of radar and the atomic bomb during the war. Both of these investments could have contributed to the consolidation of university research on the high level attained in the 1940s and 1950s and could have eased the transition to a period of relatively moderate growth. However, members of the scientific community used the orbiting of *Sputnik* for a much more comprehensive effort to advance research. They created an atmosphere of general apprehension that the United States might lose its position of scientific leadership to the Soviet Union, implying that this could have disastrous consequences for the security and prosperity of the country.[10]

This propaganda fell on fertile ground. It fitted in very well with attitudes during the Cold War, which was at its height, and it was supported by some evidence that American economic superiority (which was also at its height) was to some extent based on scientific advance (Freeman & Young, 1965, pp. 31–37, 71; Gruber, Mehta, & Vernon, 1967; Keesing, 1967). From this emerged a new approach to the support of science. Support was not to be tied to any known uses of research in education, industry, or professional services, but was to be developed as a basic resource from which these other activities were supposed to receive stimulus.

As a result the leading universities not only became "federal-grant universities," but they also became to a large extent consortiums of research institutions (Orlans, 1962). This meant that the need for academic teachers (with emphasis on teaching rather than research) and for high-level professional practitioners (occasionally engaged in research) no longer set the framework for the university. Rather, the need for research assistants began to determine the size and kinds of graduate education provided by the universities. In many cases research and graduate training became virtually in-service training programs designed to provide personnel for the expanding university research enterprise. Professors who needed assistants for their projects "recruited" graduate students to work for them and trained them as industrial firms would. The number of institutes conferring Ph.D. degrees increased from 158 in 1953–54 to 296 in 1969–70 (Harris, 1972, pp. 355, 363), and the share of the

---

[10]For some of the reactions to *Sputnik* see "News of Science" (1957*a*, 1957*b*) and DuShane (1957).

20 leading institutions granting Ph.D.'s decreased from nearly 70 percent in 1948–49 to 37 percent in 1970–71 (see Table 1 above). Over the same period, the fraction of Ph.D.'s employed in the academic system did not decrease, and perhaps even increased to some extent, in spite of the increase in the numbers of Ph.D.'s trained (see Table 4). All this shows that most of the increased Ph.D. production was geared for an internal market.

It was evident that this situation would sooner or later raise the question of how the government should determine the kinds and the amount of its support for research. Since no one could give a satisfactory answer to this question, there was a tacit agreement to avoid it.[11] This avoidance was successful for a surprisingly long time. Although the indexes of economic activity grew at a much slower pace than those of scientific research, expenditures in research, especially in university research, were a small item in the economy. Total expenditure on research and development in 1963–64 ranged from 1 to 3.4 percent of the GNP in the industrially advanced countries, between 7 to 26 percent of which went to higher education. However, in countries with high expenditures on research (2 percent or more), the share of universities was in no case higher than 13 percent (Organisation for Economic Co-operation and Development, 1967*a*, p. 14). From the point of view of the research workers, therefore, the best policy seemed to be to postpone raising the question of criteria for the support of

[11]See the letter to *Science* from V. Weisskopf, quoted in Orlans (1968, p. 115, fn. 3). The inevitability of a slowdown has been pointed out by—among others— Price (1963, p. 19).

				Ratio of shares	
	Share of employment			1964 to	1970 to
Type of employer	*1948*	*1964*	*1970*	*1948*	*1964*
N		79,372	125,234		
Educational institutions	54.5	53.1	60.0	.97	1.13
Industry	32.8	32.9	29.5	1.01	.90
Government	10.9	11.8	10.5	1.08	.89

TABLE 4 *Proportion of doctorate holders in science, social science, and engineering, by type of employment, United States, 1948–1970*

SOURCES: Freeman (1971, table 7.6A, p. 132); National Science Foundation (1971, table A-5, p. 45).

research as long as possible, and to face a reduced rate of growth from a position of greater strength.

However, this force-feeding of university research had some unexpected consequences. Since the leading universities employed increasingly large numbers of graduate students and postdoctoral fellows in full-time research and diverted to research an increasingly larger fraction of the time of their permanent academic staff, the supply of suitable graduates for teaching and industrial work would have been reduced, had the deficiency not been made up by the large increase in the number of Ph.D.'s. The share of industry and government in the employment of Ph.D.'s did not decrease very much between 1948 and 1970, (see Table 4), and that of colleges and universities previously not engaged in research probably increased. But this was accomplished only at a cost. Many institutions that used to have small or no research programs were now obliged to institute such programs to obtain teaching staff of the same quality as they used to have, and they were encouraged to do so by the availability of federal funds. Some universities also had to develop Ph.D. programs to recruit and train their research workers (see Table 1). Industrial firms felt it necessary to extend their operations beyond what was needed for their production of plans in order to obtain research and development workers of the same quality they had employed before. They could afford to do this because government was willing to compensate and even reward them for their expenses on research.

As a result, university research, which prior to the 1940s had always been linked to training Ph.D.'s for the college and the industrial and professional service markets, was now to a large extent independent from those training functions. Research became a separate operation, paid for by the federal government, that produced knowledge for the public good or for specific military or civilian purposes. Training for research was now primarily a function of the government's demand for such research.

This severed university research from both professional training (except training for research) and general education. Little attention has been paid to the possibility of *utilizing* new specialties outside the framework of research or of translating them into innovations in the liberal arts curriculum. The evidence for this may be found in suggestions by industrial firms that Ph.D.'s are overtrained (which may be a euphemism for mistrained) for industrial work, in the pronounced reluctance of junior colleges to accept Ph.D.'s, and in the recent introduction of nonresearch advanced degrees (somewhat like the French *agrégation*) designed for college teachers in general (Spurr, 1970, pp. 186–187).

Thus the force-feeding of research created in the United States a situation reminiscent of the results of direct support of research by the governments of Europe during the early years of this century and the end of the last. It created a chronic problem of how to determine the proper amount to be spent on research as well as a problem of how to integrate research with the teaching and professional training functions of the university.

THE IMPACT OF THE AMERICAN MODEL The great successes of American research during and after the Second World War had an effect on the research establishments of other countries similar to that which the great successes of German science in the second half of the nineteenth century had had. In one country after another, efforts were made—starting in the late 1950s or early 1960s—to increase investments in research at the universities and elsewhere (Mesthene, 1965). Except in Britain, where there was relatively little dissatisfaction with the quality of the universities (only a strong demand for more universities), reform of the universities was considered one of the basic conditions of improvement of the economy and society in general. The ideas of university reform included, among others, more intensive training in research, greater flexibility both in curricula and research, more organized research that stressed collegial cooperation rather than the dictatorial authority of the incumbent of the chair, increased subsidy for research through project grants to stimulate competition, and increased autonomy of the junior staff. At the same time European systems also attempted to follow the American example in increasing attendance rates at universities. Of course, numerical expansion competed for resources with the expansion of research (Organisation for Economic Co-operation and Development, 1974a, p. 39).

Even though there were no actual targets concerning the numbers and kinds of students to be trained or the amount and kinds of research to be performed, planning of both was greatly influenced by easily measurable indexes, such as the percentage of the age group (or of the population) attending institutions of higher education and the percentage of the gross national product spent on research. Both of these showed such a great gap between American (and Soviet) efforts on the one hand, and those of the Western European nations on the other,[12] that these latter countries could have had little doubt of their need to expand. Whereas the percentage of GNP spent on research in 1963–64 was 3.4 in the United States, 3 (in 1962) in the U.S.S.R., and 2.3 in Britain, the percentages in the continental countries and Japan were all below 1.9 (Freeman & Young, 1965, p. 117; Organisation for Economic Co-operation and Development, 1967*a*, p. 14).[13] A further concern was the so-called brain-drain, that is, the tendency of research workers to migrate to the United States.

Thus every country wanted to imitate the American model exactly when there emerged in that system new and not sufficiently recognized problems. The American system—as has been seen—had grown into a position of leadership through an intricate division of labor between hierarchically arranged graduate schools and colleges and between university and industrial research. However, the imitators of the American system abroad were only faintly aware of this background of American university research. Their model was the American system's exceptional effort and success during the Second World War, and its post-Sputnik boom in research. Instead of interpreting these results as the outcome of temporary mobilization, there were projections of the trend of American developments in the early 1960s into the far future (National Education Association, 1959, 1961, 1963, 1965). This created a mirage of a vast university system educating about half of the relevant age group at good institutions that conducted research at a respectable level.

As a result, an attempt was made to implant the most

---

[12] Britain did reasonably well in research, but university attendance was low there, too.

[13] This percentage gap has been closed by now. In 1973 the United States spent 2.35 percent of its GNP on research and development, compared with 2.36 in West Germany, 3.10 in the U.S.S.R., 1.73 in France, and 1.82 in Japan. The latest data for Britain—2.73 percent—are from 1969 (National Science Foundation, 1976, p. 154).

advanced type of American graduate school into European systems and—at the same time—to increase rapidly student enrollments in Europe. As has been pointed out, this process rapidly increased the fraction of students who had only vague plans for professional careers. Since in Europe only a single framework of teaching existed for an essentially professional degree, and integration of research and teaching was based on the assumption that some "overtraining" in research was useful for students entering professional careers, this new breed of students would have created stress on the system even without attempts at greater emphasis on research. Separate measures ought to have been taken to deal with the needs of the "general" student, as well as with the needs of advanced research and training for research, and attention should have been paid to the coordination of these two new functions. However, as shown in the previous chapter, there was little awareness of the problem of the general student. Thus while much of the budget was spent on the provision of rather indifferent teaching to increased numbers of unsatisfactorily prepared students, all the intellectual and organizational efforts at change in the 1960s were concerned with the creation of facilities and arrangements to improve research and graduate training. As a result, none of the functions was either adequately financed, or organized.

Under these circumstances, the efforts to increase the efficiency of university research could not have been successful. This became manifest in the late 1960s. Although the 1968–1970 university revolts had a political character that could not be attributed to the internal problems of the university, one of the roots of the revolt—and of the widespread support for it, especially among social science students—was the discrepancy between an increasingly specialized and research-oriented—yet rather superficial—instruction and the motivation of students who were interested in some kind of general education. The result was that the exclusive preoccupation with research in the 1960s was replaced by a similarly exclusive concern with the educational functions of the university. However, the new efforts have not been directed toward the improvement of the quality of teaching and education but toward increasing enrollments and satisfying students' demands for representation and participation in the governance of the universities. Therefore—apart from a few promising experiments such as the open universities—this reversal of interest has not led to a better balance between research and study.

Because of the political aims of the reforms, in many cases both teaching and research have suffered. What goes on under the name of research in some departments, especially in the arts and social sciences, is a kind of progressive educational experiment based on neo-Marxist doctrine. Students and junior staff (the latter being fairly well paid, but usually ill-prepared) conduct studies which are in fact life adjustment courses, or experiments in group decision making and leadership. Research, if conducted at all, is often part of this life adjustment curriculum. Its purpose is not the advancement of knowledge, but the exploration of some problem that by common decision of the group is considered socially important—with more attention given to obtaining results consistent with prevailing ideological fashion than to discovering new knowledge.

Of course, not all departments have been equally affected by these developments. In most of the natural science departments the effects are much less noticeable than in the social sciences and humanities. However, the relationship between research and teaching has, on balance, suffered in all fields. The research facilities have been improved at many universities, and departments that have well-qualified students oriented to serious study and research may be able to give better training to their doctoral-level students than they gave ten years ago. But even these parts of the university are under serious financial pressure due to the preemption of the budget for teaching purposes, and their morale is often undermined by time-consuming and unpleasant administrative procedures and by the political agitation that has pervaded the universities (Domes, 1976).

CONCLUSION These developments have cut short the efforts at the creation of up-to-date research universities in Europe. There have been no serious efforts at constructive restructuring of the relationship between research and teaching (although, as has been pointed out, a great deal of restructuring took place by default); attempts at the differentiation among degree levels have not been carried out consistently; and administrative reforms have often been guided by political considerations, rather than the requirements of teaching, training, and research. The resulting frustrations have reinforced the long-standing trend toward the transfer of the seat of advanced research from the universities to nonteaching research institutions, such as the Max Planck institutes in Germany, and the units of the *Centre national de la recherche scientifique* in France. Thus in a paradoxical way the aborted reform of continental European universities, which had begun as an attempt at transforming them in the image of American graduate schools, led to moving much advanced research out of the universities into specialized institutes, and to the transformation of parts of the universities into rather low-grade institutions of quasi-professional education.

The possibility of developing nonteaching research institutes is also being discussed in the United States. There university structure is adequate for advanced research, and—after initial setbacks—the system now seems to be able to deal with attempts at politicization, or, at any rate, to keep it on a level on which it does not seriously interfere with research and teaching. But there is a very serious financial problem. University research and Ph.D. employment have come to be dependent overwhelmingly on support by central government, and that support has been cut back. This was inevitable, but nevertheless, the system was entirely unprepared for it when it came. The capability of the universities to adapt themselves to renewed scarcity was further reduced by the student disturbances and by subsequent economic depression. These pressures have made adjustment particularly difficult. The actual problem is that during the days of plenty a policy was adopted according to which the government would support practically every research project submitted by qualified researchers on the recommendation of panels of recognized scientists in the field. Thus, the peer-review system assumed a policy-making function that it was never meant to perform.[14] This produced a growth rate of 25 percent in the expenditure on basic university research between 1960 and 1968 (Organisation for Economic Co-operation and Development, 1974*a*, p. 39) that would have

[14]A typical manifestation of confused thinking on this issue is the prolonged and apparently endless debate about the peer-review system. The system has been under attack for years on grounds of alleged corruption, in spite of overwhelming evidence to the contrary (Gustafson, 1975). Peer review has been effective as a mechanism of allocation of funds. The trouble is that it has been used as a mechanism of determining the level of support for science.

been unsustainable under any circumstances, and is particularly unsustainable under the present conditions of reduced economic growth. Therefore, new criteria, or more realistically, new mechanisms have to be found for the support of science on a sustainable level, that is, on a level that in the long run does not exceed the growth of the economy.

However, instead of looking for a solution to this problem, the academic community and science policy makers are still busy reacting to the trauma of the sudden change of fortunes. This foreseeable, and actually foreseen, event, gave rise to an anomic response (see Chapter 1) manifesting itself in basic doubts about the purpose and justification of scientific research, the social and political responsibility of researchers, and the contribution of research to the furtherance of social justice. All these are important issues, but largely irrelevant to the present-day difficulties of science, since those difficulties are not the result of past inattention to these issues. The salience of these issues detracts attention from the problem of stabilizing support for research and finding new mechanism of allocation, and weakens the inclination to support science altogether by raising doubts about its very justification.

Thus the future of university research is in jeopardy everywhere. This fact also diminishes the prospect of finding solutions for the problem of general education. As has been pointed out in the previous chapter, the quality and advancement of this type of education has depended on constant efforts on the part of graduates and some of the teachers of the best research universities to introduce newly created knowledge into the college curriculum. Transferring various types of advanced research to nonteaching institutions would sever this connection between advanced research and college studies and reduce the latter to studies of the secondary level.

As has been pointed out, part of the inability of the universities in coming to grips with the difficulties in carrying out their traditional mission of teaching and research is due to the fact that—under the impact of external and internal criticism and withdrawal of support—they have shifted their attention to the question of what contributions universities could make to social welfare and justice. Of course, universities have always made contributions to these ends indirectly, through the beneficial effects of the spread of scientific knowledge. But now universities are required to consider the furtherance of welfare and justice as one of their main functions, even at the cost of possible damage to their traditional functions of teaching and research. Therefore, any suggestions for the solution of the present-day difficulties of universities have to be preceded by an examination of these new demands on the university.

6. Universities, Politics, and Social Criticism

Teaching, training, and fundamental research have been the responsibility mainly of universities and related academic institutions and have been the main functions of these institutions in modern societies. Universities perform other functions, such as offering social criticism, facilitating social mobility, popularizing science and scholarship, and organizing a variety of services for members and, occasionally, for the neighboring community, but none of these are performed primarily by universities, and the role of universities in these areas may be quite limited. For example, in a working democracy, social criticism will be conducted mainly by the press and politicians, with only marginal contributions from academic people. And economically growing societies have always fostered a great deal of social mobility, irrespective of the amount of higher education.

Nonetheless, social criticism and the facilitation of social mobility have become associated with universities to such an extent that this association deeply influences government policies toward and social expectations of higher education. As has been seen in the previous chapters, all university systems have undergone politicization in recent years, and the politicization of some systems has been endemic. And, of course, as institutions training for the professions, universities are gatekeepers to some of the most desired social positions. The role of universities in social criticism will be discussed in this chapter, and their role in social mobility in Chapter 7.

ECOLOGICAL AND STRUCTURAL CONDITIONS OF CRITICISM

In most countries universities contain the greatest concentrations of intellectually gifted people in general, and of the intellectually gifted young in particular. Since these are the people most likely to reflect, speak, and write on social affairs, much of this activity will take place at universities and will be conducted by people associated with universities. Furthermore, since intelligent people are less likely to accept rationalizations of the existing state of affairs on their face value, and since young people are less attached than others to traditional views, the university population is more likely than the general population to be critical of society (Ladd & Lipset, 1975; Lipset et al., 1954, p. 1148; Schumpeter, 1947, pp. 145–155; Shils, 1972). Thus even universities that are generally sympathetic to prevailing social ideologies, or those that are deliberately nonpolitical, will contain disproportionate numbers of individuals critical of the existing state of affairs.

In Britain and the United States, universities have accepted responsibility for the education—and not only the instruction—of their students; this critical propensity of the university has been traditionally considered an educational asset. It has made the university a good training ground for democracy, because—by confronting young minds with new, unorthodox ideas—it challenges their inherited beliefs and compels them to engage in controversy, to try to understand views different from their own, and thus to adopt and defend a position based on rational consideration rather than prejudice.

In most other countries the involvement of universities in social criticism has been political, rather than educational. In countries deprived of political freedom—and few countries in Europe, and none in Asia and Latin America have not been deprived of freedom sometime in the recent past—universities often have formal or informal privileges. Academic freedom is in many countries interpreted as involving an extraterritorial right that exempts the university area from police supervision. As a result, in autocratic regimes the universities become the main centers of free political activity. In Latin American countries, which have had a long tradition of dictatorship as well as a tradition of academic extraterritoriality, there has developed a unique type of political university in which politics is almost as important as, and occasionally more important than, learning (Atcon, 1966; Silvert, 1964, pp. 206–226). This political tradition of universities also became endemic in Japan and in many countries of continental Europe, although in these countries it has not encroached upon the intellectual functions of the university to the same extent as in Latin America (Okada, 1964, p. 4; Sekine, 1975; Shimbori, 1964, 1968, 1973). Least politicized of all were the universities in Britain and the United States, because these were democratic countries and their universities were actively concerned with educating students for democracy. Although they were not concerned with democratic education, there was also little politicization in the past of Dutch, Scandinavian, and Swiss universities, apparently because there was no reason to restrict political activity to the universities in these stable democratic countries.

A new condition, which politicized universities even in well-established democracies, emerged in the 1960s. Universities attained unprecedented sizes, with student populations of tens of thousands, or even more than a hundred thousand. As direct "revolutionary" political action requires young people who have few economic responsibilities, no family encumbrances, a relative abundance of free time, and a place to meet, universities are an ideal environment for such action. Today, an increasingly high proportion of the entire age group between 18 and 22 is concentrated in universities. Previously the campus contained only potential leaders and ideologues. Today it also contains the troops needed for political action. This means that any political crisis that leads to heightened political activity, especially activity that involves violence for the attainment of political ends, is likely to originate from campuses (Archer, 1972; Lipset, 1967, 1969; Lipset & Wolin, 1965). The decline of collegiate traditions in the 1950s and 1960s described in Chapter 4 exposed even the American and British universities to political activism.

Of course, the new potential of the universities for political activity is not a sufficient condition of their politicization. It only creates an opportunity for those who want to use the university for such purposes. Thus the student disturbances of 1968 and the following years were the result of specific events—especially the Vietnam War and, in the United States, also racial conflict—and of deliberate agitation by radical groups. But their unexpected dimensions and impact were the result of the potential that had been building up unnoticed during the preceding decade.

TYPES AND DEGREES OF POLITICIZATION   At the height of the disturbances it seemed that universities all around the world would be irreversibly politicized. Today the situation is much less clear. Some university faculties in Europe have become virtually ideological indoctrination centers (as departments of economics and of social science have been for a long time in some Japanese and Latin American universities), and others have returned to their pre-1968 low-level political activity. The majority are somewhere in between; there is little interference with research and teaching, but in Europe and Japan there are strongly entrenched left-wing groups that dominate student unions or parts of the university, control the political posture of the university, and keep open the option of using the university as a basis of renewed activism (Domes, 1976; Johnson, 1975).

It is impossible to predict the future course of events, since that will be decided to a large extent by general political conditions. But one can analyze the situation today and try to understand the mechanisms that produce different types and degrees of politicization.

The greatest and most permanent politicization has occurred in Latin America, Italy, Japan, and in scattered places elsewhere. This politicization consists of attempts by radical groups in the universities to enforce certain political views by more or less open discrimination and pressures (frequently including violence) against recalcitrants, particularly in politically sensitive fields.[1] The background of this seems to be a tradition of religious or ideological control of higher education by political and church authorities. There was, in these countries, a basic inconsistency in the policies toward universities. On the one hand, governments tried to keep a tight rein on political dissent at the universities, but, on the other hand, they conferred political immunities on university students and teachers that encouraged the use of the university as a preserve of dissident politics. Furthermore, the crudeness and datedness of officially endorsed ideology (and all officially endorsed ideologies become crude and dated after a short while) made dissent among intellectuals popular. Finally, the need to act in secret, to be constantly on guard, and to resist ruthless oppression, made the survival of other than well-organized, usually radical,

---

[1] There are many more cases in which political views are forced upon faculties and students by authoritarian governments of the left or the right. But this book is concerned only with ideological terror created within universities by their own teachers and students. Of course, such internal terror may lead to external, governmental, terror, either through the political victory of the groups initiating intrauniversity terror, or through outside political reaction against political agitation within the universities.

groups unlikely. Under such conditions there arose a tendency to identify "intellectual" with "political radical" (Lipset, 1967, pp. 10–12; Pipes, 1961). This identification began in eighteenth century France; there, however, dissident intellectuals could survive outside the university better than in it. But in the late nineteenth or early twentieth century, in Russia, Japan, Latin America, Italy, and—to a lesser extent—also elsewhere in continental Europe, the radical intellectual was usually also a student or a professor.

The existence of such an entrenched tradition of academic radicalism enhances the attractiveness of radical movements for students and young teachers, who are under considerable stress because they have to prove themselves through intellectual attainments. Joining radical movements reduces this stress by conferring on them the status of intellectuals without requiring proof of scholarship.[2] Those who join radical movements also enter an inner academic circle, which includes some important names and which confers prestige and provides support at the university. Widespread unemployment, or fear of unemployment, among university graduates has been another cause of their searching for a feeling of belonging and security. If, as a result, political groups of certain persuasions succeed in dominating entire systems or institutions of higher education, such as in some Latin American countries, Italy, or West Berlin, then students and academic intellectuals become a veritable social class that pursues its own politics, much like the medieval clergy in its time.

These endemic states of politicization have three characteristics: a history of political and ideological coercion inconsistently combined with the conferral of certain immunities on the universities, thus turning them into centers of conspiratorial politics; a cultural tradition of intellectual radicalism with a history, myths, heroes, and symbols of its own that originates

---

[2] This is not to say that those who join radical movements are the intellectually inferior students and young scholars. Some of the most able are also insecure. But subsequent professional or academic success seems to reduce radicalism, except, of course, if radicalism becomes fashionable or dominant. Then people remain or become radical out of opportunism.

However, it has to be stressed that few intellectuals will be outright conservatives under any circumstances. Their interest in analysis and discovery is compatible with conservatism only with a great many qualifications.

in the above circumstances but becomes an independent factor subsequently;[3] and a high degree of institutional support of this tradition through organized student movements and ideological or political cliques controlling university departments, entire universities, and/or the mass media.

In countries in which the first of these conditions—the reinforcement of radicalism through inconsistent oppression—has been absent for a long time, politicization, as has been pointed out, is not endemic. But the existence of an international cultural tradition of intellectual radicalism is a permanent attraction for the young and the insecure also in these countries. The extreme swings from almost universal radicalism to equally widespread political apathy suggest that this is a phenomenon like fashion.[4] Its attractiveness depends on the characteristics of those who originate the ideological trend and of those who follow and adopt it. An ideology—like clothes—becomes attractive only if it identifies the follower with the elite or the center. Thus, as long as fascism thrived only in Italy, it had little attraction for intellectuals elsewhere. But with the rise of nazism in the German universities—which were the leading academic institutions in the world—nazism spread like bushfire. But for the coincidence, on the one hand, that Jews—who were overrepresented among intellectuals in Europe—were used as scapegoats in the Nazi ideology and, on the other hand, that American and English universities still possessed a tradition of enlightened and liberal Christianity as well as a great deal of not-so-enlightened belief in their social superiority, the appeal of nazism would have been even more widespread.

This interpretation is also consistent with the recent rise of left-wing ideologies. They had been widespread among Japa-

[3] The contents of the radical tradition may change. In the thirties fascism had the same irresistible attraction to many students all over the world as radical left ideologies have today. In fact, the difference between extreme right and extreme left is often purely semantic. I know of one case in the United States in which a black militant instructor in a college known for its liberal sympathies used the summary of Nazi anti-Jewish propaganda—described in a history of the extermination of the Jews in Europe—as a factual source on the character of the Jews.

[4] It has to be emphasized that I am speaking here only of the swings of ideological fashion among intellectuals and the related attempts at the usurpation of the university for political purposes, and not about the creation or adoption of ideologies in general. The creation and adoption of ideologies are in themselves psychologically and sociologically necessary, and potentially useful, processes.

nese and Latin American students during the fifties and early sixties without having had much influence elsewhere. But when radical leftism became popular in the leading American and European universities, there was an immediate chain reaction all over the world. The fashionlike character of this reaction is evident from the fact that the American race issue and the Vietnam war—important problems for the American students, but remote issues for the others—were central issues of the student activists everywhere. Another evidence of this fashionlike character of the movement is that the same set of symbols is used by people with totally different interests and views. For example, the so-called radical left today includes Marxists and anarchists interested in the creation of a socialist utopia of all races and nations, as well as extreme racists and nationalists for whom the hatred of certain out-groups is a central and sacred part of their political beliefs, as it was for the Nazis. Thus many autocratic regimes are considered leftist today, probably for no other reason than their opposition to such symbols as "capitalism," "imperialism," "colonialism," "liberal democracy," or—strangely enough—even "fascism" and "racism" (which they admire and practice). The use of these words is purely symbolic, since there is no attempt to verify the relationship between these terms and reality.

The propensity to adopt radical fashions is also related to social characteristics. Fashions in general are followed by the leisure classes, whose sense of security allows them to experiment and try out everything exciting, and the socially insecure, who need the reassurance of belonging to a prestigious group and of being identified with symbols conferring prestige. Investigations of the incidence of radical student activism and support of such activism by teachers are consistent with these hypotheses. Thus activism and faculty support for it in the United States were highest in the elite colleges and top universities (Ladd & Lipset, 1975, p. 142; Peterson & Bilorusky, 1971, pp. 53–55). And individual participation and support were highly correlated with indexes of insecurity, such as overall dissatisfaction, changes in religious association, and minority status (Carnegie Commission, 1972, pp. 92–93; Ladd & Lipset, 1975, pp. 163, 178). Another source of insecurity is the presence of large numbers of students in search of moral and social experience. There is some indication that such groups are concentrated in both the elite institutions, in which upwardly mobile students meet with upper-class students who can afford a great deal of experimentation with life-styles and fashions (and may be threatened with downward mobility), and in mass institutions that absorb large numbers of relatively unsuccessful students who have vague aspirations but no clear professional purpose. On the other hand, one would not expect to find many students interested in politicizing universities attending professional schools or in institutions catering to students with clearly defined intellectual or narrowly defined vocational purposes, or to students with fundamentalist religious beliefs. For the United States there is statistical evidence on the relation between size and the combination of size and quality, on the one hand, and student activism, on the other, that is consistent with this interpretation (Peterson and Bilorusky, 1971, pp. 40–49, 54). Impressionistically this hypothesis is also supported by the pattern of student disturbances in Britain and Japan.

However, institutions that have an intensive and effective educational program capable of handling the problems of their students or that sustain a communication between student and teachers, with the latter representing consistent educational principles, have often succeeded in dealing with strong currents of student radicalism without undergoing even a temporary politicization. Thus American liberal arts colleges, or academies of music (that train students individually) everywhere, were fairly successful in dealing with the wave of disturbances of the late sixties and early seventies (Peterson & Bilorusky, 1971, pp. 76–82), although such colleges have many students in search of moral and social experience and are highly susceptible to ideological fashions.

An important condition of differing susceptibilities to such fashions is the strength of scientific and professional traditions of different fields and at different institutions. In fields and in countries in which the scientific tradition has been weak, the usurpation of the university for political purposes has been easier than in fields and countries with a strong scientific tradition. This proposition is supported by the ease with which relatively nontechnical fields, such as sociology and anthropology, have been politicized, compared with the relative imperviousness to politicization of the natural and applied sciences (Peterson & Bilorusky, 1971, p. 21). Furthermore, such phenomena as turning the study of sociology, politics, or economics into an introduction to Marxist dogma occurred only in universities where the social science traditions were weak. In the United States, and even in England and France, where traditions of social research have been strong, the politicization of entire fields was avoided even in such universities as Berkeley, the London School of Economics, or the universities of Paris, in which student radicalism reached its peak. Social science has been replaced by Marxist dogma at the Free University of Berlin, in some Japanese departments of economics, and in other places lacking strong research traditions in the social sciences.

While students can start disturbances, long-term politicization of institutions requires further conditions. Students come and go, and are thus unable to influence an institution permanently. Long-term political usurpation of a university will occur only when radical groups can establish a lasting hold on parts of it. Traditionally, they have tried to do this through capturing student organizations. This is relatively easy, because the large majority of students are totally inexperienced and are not actively interested in politics (Johnson, 1975; Worms, 1967). However, student organizations have little prestige and influence in the universities and are also threatened with impermanence because of the constant flow of students.

Some permanence in student politics has been established in Europe and Japan through national and international student organizations. Situated outside the universities, these build up a permanent bureaucracy that—if supported by activists at the universities—can perpetuate itself, effectively manipulate official resolutions, and use the name of the entire national student body, or that of a particular university, for its own propagandistic purposes. But only on rare occasions can it mobilize students to political action or exert influence on the academic activities of the university.

The effective way to turn the university, or part of it, into a political tool is through substantial help from at least some of the faculty. This aid is particularly effective in continental European or Japanese universities in which every "chair" is a law unto itself. It is always possible for a political group to capture one or two chairs, to see to it that they remain under its control, and then to use the captured chairs as power bases to broaden its influence. Something like this seems to have happened in German and Japanese universities (Domes, 1976; Sekine, 1975).

In continental Europe, the powers conferred on students in university government made possible, with the cooperation of a minority of the faculty, the politicization of entire universities. It will be interesting to see the results of the 1968 arrangements in France. They confer on students considerable powers of participation, but at the same time they may considerably enhance personal contacts between students and teachers and intensify methods of instruction. Thus on the one hand they open the way to the takeover of institutions by politically active and organized groups, but on the other hand they may weaken the predisposition of students to join the activists by providing them with alternative contacts and with a more satisfactory educational experience.[5]

These considerations explain why most countries have not seen a complete political usurpation of their universities, but rather different degrees of politicization, ranging from practically none to politicization of parts of the university, and to "latent" politicization. In the last, political groups obtain decisive power—by such means as capturing the university administration—thus creating for themselves a permanent option to mobilize the university for their purposes, but refrain—at least temporarily—from open interference in teaching and research.

If these speculations are correct, the prospects that social criticism at universities will again be used for democratic education, without interfering with inspired learning and research, are not good. Even if universities are not usurped for political purposes, they will be more sensitive to political currents and more prone to react to them with a noise not conducive to democratic education and to scholarship, or with outbursts of political activism and violence. There is also a constant possibility of insidious conversion of universities into party institutions.

[5] So far, prospects for this happening do not appear very good (see Bourricaud, 1975), probably because of the meager resources and lack of academic leadership in the universities.

This conclusion suggests that the traditional attitude to the political function of the university has to be revised. When the idea that the university is, and should be, a place of social criticism emerged in Britain and the United States, universities were safely remote from the centers of political struggle. The danger that their academic activities might be influenced by that struggle was negligible, and the possibility that political pronouncements at the universities might influence actual policies was remote. Under those conditions it was reasonable to treat the university as a place where irreverent and even frivolous and irresponsible political views could be propagated, since it was taken for granted that they would not have any immediate political impact. This is an untenable position today—as it has been for a long time in continental Europe—because now universities are actually, or potentially, an important political force. Organized university politics is no longer children's game, but serious politics. Allowing organized students and teachers to use the university for political purposes amounts to tolerating the rise of a privileged class that can divert public resources allocated for other purposes to the furtherance of its own political interests. It is as inconsistent with democratic principles as allowing civil servants to use their offices and paid time for party politics and propaganda.

This is not to recommend the suppression or even voluntary avoidance of free critical thought and speech on political issues on campuses, or even to recommend abstinence from political activities on campus. Such a recommendation would be both unrealistic and unjustified. Teachers have a right to engage in politics, as do all other citizens. And to prevent students from taking an active interest in politics in their formative years would stunt their development as autonomous individuals and responsible citizens, in addition to being a violation of their rights.

But political debate and activity have to be regulated by two principles: namely, that every university activity has to be consistent with the aims of the university as an institution of research and teaching, and that members of universities must not have political privileges not accorded to other citizens.

Accordingly, a distinction has to be made between political discussion and organized political activity. The former has a place at the university—and not only as political science—since the formation of political opinions is an essential part of the educational process. But only as part of the educational process has it a place at the university; otherwise the university becomes a publicly supported partisan institution, which is inconsistent with democratic principle as well as with the dispassionate pursuit of science and learning. This means that without expecting university politics to be more scientific than real politics, one can expect it to be intellectually more honest and detached than the latter.

This would mean, for example, the disallowance of political speeches or lectures that limit admission according to political criteria, that do not have an impartial chairman, or that do not give satisfactory assurances for a fairly administered period of questions and answers. Many universities have rules of this kind, but they are usually not enforced, the prevailing view being that they are unenforceable. It seems, however, that the difficulty of enforcement is primarily due to the negative approach of the universities to this matter. As has been pointed out, since the fifties and sixties American and British universities have given low priority to their extracurricular educational functions (and other systems have never cared about them). They pay no, or little, attention to the organization of political and other public discussions, leave them to assistant deans with little academic status or to the students themselves, do not care what happens in them, and are alerted only when serious disciplinary problems arise. Under such circumstances it is no surprise that there is little respect for the rules of intellectually honest debate, since those rules come to attention only in the negative context of "law enforcement." Thus students develop the same disrespect for the laws of honest debate as slum dwellers, whose only experiences with law come from encounters with the police, have for laws in general. If universities wish to improve the tone of university politics and to pay more than lip service to the critical function of the university, then they have to pay much more positive attention to this problem. They have to involve in these matters members with high university status, community organizations, and perhaps college newspapers, and plan campus debates imaginatively and carefully (as, indeed, some colleges do). Above all, they have to insist on responsible political behavior on the part of their teachers.

As to the organization of political activity on campus, that should be strictly limited to internal clublike activities. No organized political action involving those other than members of the academic community should be centered on campus or originate from it. This is not to discourage political activity among members of the academic community, but to encourage them to engage in such activities as citizens and not as a privileged elite.

It seems that the adoption of this kind of policy is necessary if the independence and integrity of the universities as institutions of learning is to be preserved in an age when the overwhelming majority of politically active young people are concentrated at institutions of higher education. Of course, this policy may not always be easy to enforce. The overwhelming majority of teachers and students, however, do not go to universities to engage in political activism, but to work and to study. Their proneness to disturbance and subversion is to some extent the result of an absence of clear rules of conduct. This lack of clarity causes confusion that is easily exploited by those who want to usurp the universities for political purposes. Clarification of principles does not automatically ensure their enforcement, but it is a necessary condition of that enforcement.

CONCLUSION Universities all over the world are faced with the choice between being chronically threatened by politicization or actively regulating political activity in their midst. Such regulation would involve an educational responsibility that universities outside Britain and the United States have never accepted, and that British and American universities have tended to abandon since the 1950s.

With a few exceptions in the United States, the tendency is to prefer living with the chronic threat, rather than to accept new educational responsibilities. This alternative seems to be more convenient and—as the experience of continental Europe shows—it has allowed long periods of reasonably productive work at the cost of violent, but short-run, upheavals. It is questionable, however, whether past experience is, in this case, a valid guide for the future. There are much larger numbers of students today—in absolute terms as well as proportionately—and their need for education, as distinct from instruction, is greater than in the past. The political potential of the universities has increased concomitantly with the growth of enrollments, and so has the propensity of political parties and civil servants to use this potential for their own purposes. Therefore, the cost of living with the threat of politicization may increase considerably, and interference with research and teaching may become intolerable. Even now the amount of time spent on compliance with political processes (such as "codetermination" in Europe) or politically inspired administrative procedures (such as "equal opportunity" in the United States) is often a serious encroachment on the time available for research and teaching (not to speak of the direct damage caused by some of these procedures).

Furthermore, politicization of the university is not only a threat to science and learning, but also to freedom and democracy. A publicly supported, politicized university is a source of political privilege that can be used for the circumvention and subversion of democracy and—judging from the precedents— the subsequent curtailment of freedom of teaching and research in politically sensitive fields. Therefore, the only alternative consistent with the traditional university functions of research and teaching is the regulation of political activity on campus by the university. Since this is part of the university's responsibility for education in general, the possibilities for such regulation will be discussed in the final chapter, after discussing the role of universities in the promotion of social equality, another university function that has gained prominence in recent years.

7. Universities, Social Justice, and Equality

The role of universities in the furtherance of social justice, like their role in social criticism, has been a secondary one. Equality of rights, duties, and opportunities has to be ensured in all institutions of society, and putting the main burden of furthering social justice on the universities is as much an indication of social inequality in society at large as regarding the universities as the main centers of social criticism is an indication of oppression.

But while the university as an institution does not engage in social criticism—only individuals connected with it do—it has an institutional responsibility for the furtherance of social justice. It trains students for the professions, is an important channel of mobility into various elite positions, and is the most important place to acquire higher learning. By allowing or preventing discrimination in admissions and study, the university harms or safeguards social justice.[1]

In historical perspective, universities have done moderately well. In spite of recurrent charges that educational systems preserve class privileges, education has probably been one of the least discriminatory institutions of any society. This is not to say that there is no discrimination based on social class. Children of the poor are made to feel inferior to those of the rich and powerful in many subtle and occasionally brutal ways. Above all, the wealthy can buy education for their children and the poor cannot. But while the recognition of individual achievement has been a norm inherent in institutions of education, discrimination on the basis of class originates in the

---

[1] There is also a problem of discrimination in the hiring of faculty and staff, but that is not different from discrimination in any other kind of employment.

political and economic sector and intrudes from there into education, as it does into everything else. It is often perceived as corrupting education, even in societies that otherwise accept the legitimacy of social class distinctions. Thus, although universities have not risen very far above the societies to which they belong, relative to their societies they have usually adopted open-minded, nondiscriminatory practices.

If, nonetheless, universities have been accused of discrimination, this has not been because they discriminate against certain groups more than other institutions, but because even slight discrimination is perceived as incongruent with the norms and values of the university. What is tolerated elsewhere is intolerable at the universities.

EQUALITY OF OPPORTUNITY FOR HIGHER EDUCATION In modern times the main obstacle to achieving social justice in the universities has been the unintentional discrimination against lower classes. Deliberate discrimination on the basis of class background was abolished in all modern university systems during the nineteenth century. But few efforts were made to overcome the educational handicaps of youth from the lower classes. The handicap was attributed to economic causes, and attempts to correct it consisted of the provision of free tuition, scholarships, dormitories, and so on. With the rise of the welfare state in the 1940s, governments accepted responsibility for the provision of this support and ensured—more or less effectively—that no one admitted to a university would be prevented from studying because of poverty. The elimination of economic handicaps revealed, however, that the roots of educational differences were not purely economic. Lower-class youth continued to drop out early from the educational process even in countries that provided adequate support at universities for every person.

A number of studies in the 1950s and 1960s investigated this problem of educational inequality among children and students from different class backgrounds. (See, for example, Ben-David, 1963–64; Duncan, 1968; Floud, Halsey, & Martin, 1956; Halsey, Floud, & Anderson, 1961, pp. 209–240; Kahl, 1959, pp. 276–298; Poignant, 1969, pp. 195–202; and Sewell & Shah, 1967). These studies took it for granted that ability as measured by tests was a necessary condition of educational attainment, and they investigated the causes of differences in educational attainment of youth of equal ability. Most of the findings point to the importance of conditions preceding university entrance: The handicap of lower-class children became evident much earlier than in college, and the educational success and aspirations of children are related to class background for a variety of reasons not sufficiently understood. This is not to say that the educational system has no effect on educational equality. It was found that systems—such as the traditional European systems—that tried to identify the abilities of pupils at an early age and streamed them into schools appropriate to their abilities were less favorable to the advancement of lower-class students than systems in which selection occurred later, as in the United States and—since the Second World War—in Japan. Systems providing a greater variety of curricula and types and levels of study, and in which instruction was more intensive, such as those in the United States, Britain, and the U.S.S.R., were more successful in educating lower-class students than the more homogeneous European universities, in which the student was given few choices and was largely left to his own resources.

These investigations had a great impact on educational policy. In Europe efforts were made to extend educational opportunity in every country. These efforts concentrated on the variables that—according to the previously mentioned studies—were manipulatable: namely, on formal education. High school education was considerably liberalized, which created within a short time a greatly increased pool of candidates formally qualified to enter universities and led to rapid increases in university attendance (Organisation for Economic Co-operation and Development, 1971, pp. 97–119). The participation of students from the lower classes in higher education also increased everywhere. Thus the ratio of the percentage of students from the lowest socioeconomic category to the percentage of male active population in the same category has somewhat increased everywhere, and that of the highest socioeconomic category decreased everywhere in Europe during the 1960s (Organisation for Economic Co-operation and Development, 1971, pp. 48–49). There was throughout the sixties an active drive to make higher education more flexible, much of which was stimulated by the research on the participation of youth from different classes in higher education undertaken in the 1950s and early 1960s (Organisation for Economic Co-operation and

Development, 1974*b*). This drive was characterized mainly by the promotion to university status of technical institutes, teacher-training colleges, and similar institutions of postsecondary education. Another means, numerically of much smaller significance, was the Open University in Britain, and now also elsewhere, which catered to part-time students through broadcast lectures and concentrated courses. But advance toward equality was slower than expected. Probably part of the reason was that the reforms on the European continent were concerned mainly with increasing the numbers of students through easing the requirements for examinations and introducing new types of study and paid little attention to the qualifications of teachers or the quality of teaching on all levels. In Britain and the United States, where education was more intensive, there was, indeed, somewhat less inequality among the classes than in continental Europe.[2]

There was also less inequality in at least one Communist country, Yugoslavia (Organisation for Economic Co-operation and Development, 1971, pp. 48–49), and probably also in others. But that was attained by a drastic manipulation of the educational system, the cost of which—in terms of low educational standards and individual dissatisfaction—was very great (Organisation for Economic Co-operation and Development, 1970, p. 14). Therefore, it is difficult to use these results as standards of comparison for Western European countries.

Compared to Europe, the situation in the United States was much better, although differences in educational attainment due to social background continued to exist there as well (Sewell & Shah, 1967). Because these differences often coincided with differences in race, and because there was a high cultural sensitivity to inequality, the problem in the United States was politically much more acute than in Europe, in spite of impressive advances in the reduction of educational inequalities in general, and between races in particular (Duncan, 1968; Hauser, 1976). The main problem has been the very high correlation between IQ and social class (Folger, Astin, & Bayer, 1970, p. 308), which—at least for the present—cannot be reduced by university or even high school reform. Thus the expectation

[2] For some comparisons of cost per student in different countries, see Organisation for Economic Co-operation and Development (1974*c*, p. 208).

that educational reform would eliminate differences between the educational attainments of youth coming from different classes in a decade or two has been simply unrealistic. However, the failure of reforms has not given rise to a more realistic level of aspiration or to the adoption of a more tentative, experimental approach to the improvement of the educational potential and attainments of lower-class children. Such a conclusion would be politically unpopular, particularly in the United States, where the class problem is also a racial one, and people press for policies with visible and immediate effects. Thus the reaction to the disappointingly slow progress toward equality has been an attempt to redefine the concept of social justice. Since the late 1960s "equal opportunity" in higher education (and in employment) has ceased to mean equal *access* for equally qualified individuals, irrespective of race, class, or religion. Instead many people have interpreted it as the proportional *achievement* of *groups* defined by class, race, ethnicity, sex, or—potentially—any other criterion, if those falling within a category are interested in defining themselves politically. This new view, which refuses to distinguish between equality of opportunity and equality of outcome, has been particularly influential in the United States, where it has actually affected official policy in education and employment. But the idea is also influential elsewhere and exerts a pressure on higher education.[3]

This view changes the whole concept of social justice from one of equal individual citizenship to one of equal representation of politically defined groups. Thus, the problem of educational equality within a single society is conceived as analogous to that of educational equality among nations. This latter problem is long-standing, and the lessons that can be learned from it are relevant to the evaluation of the new demand for intrasocietal educational equality.

EDUCATIONAL EQUALITY AMONG NATIONS The problem of equality in education among nations goes back to the eighteenth century. At that time all other countries were educationally backward compared to France and England. In the nineteenth century a new dimension was added to the problem as a result of nationalism in multiethnic empires. In

---

[3] See for example the speech of Mr. Gerald Fowler, British Minister of State for Higher Education, in the Symposium on Reform and Planning of Higher Education, Oxford, 31 March–5 April in Conseil de l'Europe (1974, p. 2).

Russia and the Austro-Hungarian empire, and even more in the colonies of the large European empires, the main divisions of society were not along class but ethnic lines. In all these societies, the problem of educational justice was complicated by that of cultural and, in some, racial domination. Individual mobility was either impossible because of legal or other official barriers, or it was possible only at the cost of changing one's language, religion, cultural heritage, or nationality.

Some individuals were willing to pay this price, especially when the price was not exorbitant (the Austrianization of Czechs living in Vienna before the First World War is an example). But in many cases the price was high, and in the colonial empires, and for some minorities, such as Jews in most European or Middle Eastern countries or native Americans or American blacks, individual mobility beyond a certain level was impossible at any price.

Educational mobility in these cases was blocked in three ways: by legal-political discrimination; by the difficulty of studying in a foreign language and in the intellectual setting of a foreign culture; and by the image of cultural inferiority that affected one's self-confidence and lowered one's aspiration. Therefore, educational mobility was not treated in terms of equality of individual opportunity, but of equality of opportunity for the group as a whole. Every case of subjection had different combinations of these conditions, and each needed a different solution. But because of the limitations of human inventiveness, early solutions were adopted in subsequent situations, even if they were not originally entirely satisfactory or did not quite fit later circumstances.

The typical method of attempting to create equal opportunity throughout the nineteenth century was to arouse a combination of cultural and political nationalism. Intellectuals created movements for the cultivation of national language, literature, and history as a basis for either cultural and political independence from, or equality with, the dominant countries, or both. This constituted an opportunity for advancement for lower-class intellectuals and potentially increased the opportunity for lower-class youth, for whom study in a foreign language was a greater barrier to obtaining a good education than for young people from the upper classes.

The model was Germany. Although Germany was not dominated by foreigners in the eighteenth century, the German
nation was politically divided into numerous states. This
nation, one of the largest in Europe, had less power than the
British and the French. The rulers of some of the German states,
especially of Prussia, made great efforts to catch up with those
countries politically and economically, but in education and
culture they followed France. French education was considered
the key to the high culture of the age, just as a European
education in general would become the key to the high culture
of the nineteenth and twentieth centuries for the peoples of
Asia and Africa, or for the Jews, an Asian people dispersed
throughout Europe and the Middle East. Only those—like
Alexander von Humboldt—who gained international recognition, which meant recognition in leading French circles, were
considered first-rate intellectuals. Those who addressed themselves to the German public alone were almost by definition
second-rate even in their own country. German intellectuals
and writers in the second half of the eighteenth century made
great efforts to overcome this disability, which was finally
removed when—following the defeat of the German states and
the occupation of some of them by Napoleon in the beginning
of the nineteenth century—the rulers of Prussia realized that
cultural independence from France, and even cultural resent-
ment toward it, were useful for the struggle for national libera-
tion. The result was the reform of the German universities,
which eventually made German the main language of science
and scholarship, and in which the cultivation of German philosophy, language, and literature were given great prominence
(Brunschwig, 1974; Schnabel, 1959).

This pattern was repeated with slight variations in Italy,
Hungary, Poland, Russia, Japan, and a great many other countries. In Italy, Hungary, and parts of Poland the rebellion was
directed against the domination by German culture. The relatively unified European literary-philosophical culture broke
into a conglomeration of national cultures. This led to the
foundation of new universities and high schools, or the reformation of old ones all over Europe during the nineteenth century; in Japan in the late nineteenth century; and in this century
in other Asian countries and the Middle East. Poems and novels

were written in national languages in which little had been written before, and these languages and literatures became subjects of academic study. When these nations became independent, they established their own legal systems, giving rise to another field of academic study as well as a profession. Recently—with the academizing of social sciences—the study of the social structure and the position of new nations or of groups of nations—such as African or Latin American ones—has been added to the list of academic studies directly related to the aim of attaining cultural equality between new and old nations.

This created new intellectual, literary, and professional careers and brought the emerging intellectual classes to something like symbolic equality with the intellectuals of the culturally most advanced countries. Thus at the end of the eighteenth and early nineteenth centuries German writers and philosophers, like Goethe, Schiller, Kant, and Hegel, became international figures equal in fame to the great French writers and philosophers of the preceding era. No other group of intellectuals could quite repeat the German success, but most European countries and several Asian ones established autonomous scientific, scholarly, and literary communities that have taken their place alongside the English, French, and German communities.

The initiators and direct beneficiaries of this academic upgrading of national cultures were the local intellectuals. Nationalization of the language and some of the contents of higher education conferred on them a monopoly. In such fields as language, literature, history, law, and social science they became leading authorities. Of course, they had been authorities in these fields before, but their knowledge had not been a source of status as long as their national culture was not recognized as at least symbolically or potentially equivalent to metropolitan cultures. Symbolic upgrading of local cultures has raised automatically the status of local intellectuals in their own societies as well as abroad.

The question of benefit to society in general is a more complex one. General benefits may be of two kinds: improvement of the quality of national culture, and the facilitation of the educational mobility of individuals.

It is obvious that symbolic upgrading is not tantamount to

actual improvement of a culture. There is a world of difference between the paradigmatic case of Germany, where such upgrading followed an impressive upswing of local culture, and the many subsequent cases in which symbolic upgrading was accomplished by purely political means without much prior improvement of the local culture. Indeed, in some cases, especially in Africa and India, partly because of the difficulty in organizing and interpreting local heritage in a way suitable for its use as a background to and subject of humanistic studies, and partly because of the pluralism of local ethnic traditions, English or French has been retained as the language of instruction and as the main medium of literary and historical education. And the study of foreign languages as a preparation for a higher education in which the student has to use foreign language sources is greatly stressed in Japan, Israel, and many other countries.

It is difficult to compare the countries in which the local language was adopted in academic instruction and research and in which the local culture became the central part of humanistic education with those that retained their links with foreign cultures. The adoption of local languages for the empirical sciences and mathematics has been a liability. These fields are international; they need a language that is understood by all; and they have had one since antiquity. It was first Greek, then Arabic, followed by Latin, Italian, French, German, and English. Those who study and practice science beyond a rudimentary level need to be proficient in the current international language. The popular study of science in different local languages is possible, and it is possible that thinking and talking about science in one's mother tongue increases one's creativity, in which case the use of a national language would contribute to the level of local science, its international status, and ultimately to the cultural status of the entire group. But there is no unequivocal evidence of this. On the other hand, there is the possibility that "nationalized" science becomes parochial and backward, doing more harm than good to the group as a whole. Examples of this were the spread of romantic *Naturphilosophie* in Germany in the early nineteenth century, partly in reaction to the quantitative, exact "French" approach, and the rise of Lysenkoism in the Soviet Union in a period of extreme cultural chauvinism.

The justification of nationalizing literature, literary-histori-
cal, and social studies seems obvious. It is much more difficult
to become a writer in a foreign language than in one's mother
tongue, and the study of literary and historical documents, or
current social problems, requires mastery of the national language. Furthermore, in these fields there is a wide lay public,
proficient only in the national language, that is interested in the
results of literary and scholarly work.

This is not to say, however, that education based in the
national language is an unequivocal blessing for the group as a
whole even in these fields. Local literary and historical heritage
may be poor, in which case its academizing may lend unde-
served respect to poor standards and a narrow outlook. Therefore, in these fields, too, the long-term intellectual harm may be
greater than the short-term bliss that attends a rise in the status
of local culture.

The condition that determines whether the nationalization of
academic life will contribute to the quality of the culture is
whether local intellectuals have proved themselves in competition with their metropolitan colleagues and have attained international level prior to nationalization. This success was conspicuous among late-eighteenth-century and early-nineteenth-
century German intellectuals. Their struggle for equality of
intellectual esteem had begun much earlier than the national
struggle against Napoleonic domination, and they had had to
prove themselves against universalistic criteria.

In other cases, however, the struggle for cultural independence has started at the same time as the struggle for national
independence, or even later. This was the case in most places in
Asia, Africa, and Latin America. These conditions do not favor
the rise of universalistic standards, since the claim for cultural
independence is based not on the intrinsic quality of the
achievements of local intellectuals and scholars, but on extraneous political considerations. This standard does not breed
motivation for intellectual excellence and may actually create a
vested interest among local intellectuals to keep out—by political arguments and means—foreign cultural influence that
might expose their incompetence. Cultural parochialism will be
justified by appeals to popular sentiments of xenophobia.

Japan's success in assimilating Western learning while insisting on cultural independence as part of its bid for political equality with the large Western powers is an apparent contradiction to this hypothesis. But a closer inspection shows that the contradiction is not real. A tradition of effective study and self-improvement had existed prior to the reform of Japanese education; it was not created by the formality of establishing universities. And no one in Japan dreamed that once academic institutions were established Japanese scientists could claim a status equal to, say, contemporary German or British scientists. If anything, the Japanese have been overly reluctant to make such claims, insisting that the achievements of their scientists be judged according to the strictest international standards. Thus the educational development in Japan in many respects preceded the struggle for international political equality (Dore, 1965).

The harm done to nations by cultural nationalism is rarely recognized. The population as a whole identifies with the struggles of the intellectuals because they are under the false impression that the latter represent the popular cause. In colonial or other situations of dominance, the population lacks an awareness of internal class differences. Members of the dominated group have a feeling of internal equality, because differences within the group appear insignificant when compared to the external status disabilities of the entire group. And in some cases the differences within the group may actually be small, because of its generally oppressed and undifferentiated state. Therefore, local nationalist intellectuals are supported as if there were complete conformity between their interests and those of the populace at large.[4]

However, this situation changes the moment higher education is nationalized. Inevitably, an internal differentiation takes

[4]The price paid for cultural nationalism has never been properly assessed. Nor has it ever been stated that this price is paid by the common people to support an intellectual-professional class in its endeavor to exclude foreign intellectual competition through a variety of protectionist practices, including the spread of prejudice against foreign cultures, or even foreign languages (the famous German philosopher, Fichte, was a pioneer in this form of protectionism). Some idea of these costs can be gained from discussions of unemployment among university graduates; see Kotschnig (1937) and, on Italy, Barbagli (1974). For a view of cultural nationalism as a movement of intellectuals intent on obtaining a monopoly of the local market see Weber (1947, p. 179).

place that sets the leading intellectuals, many of whom become professional academics, apart from the rest of the populace. The intellectuals and academics are likely to transform themselves into a self-perpetuating status group, with the effect of reducing educational mobility and conceivably giving rise to greater educational injustice than under the domination of a more universalistic metropolitan culture.

INCREASED POLITICIZATION OF THE STRUGGLE FOR EDUCATIONAL EQUALITY Until the 1950s there were only a few instances of open and programmatic adoption of political or nationalistic criteria, or both, in higher learning. European fascism and some versions of communism in the 1920s and 1930s made some attempts to deny universal standards in science, but they had relatively little impact. These attempts were half-hearted and were hindered in all the relevant countries by groups of mathematicians and natural scientists who were unwilling to suppress universalistic standards or who were willing to do so only in fields other than their own.

This situation changed in the 1960s. The establishment of politically ruled international cultural organizations, first and foremost UNESCO, created an atmosphere in which standards of science and scholarship could be usurped by politically appointed representatives of states. In totalitarian countries, especially in those without a tradition of science and scholarship, these appointees frequently lacked proper qualifications. The official international forum lent a make-believe intellectual legitimacy (since UNESCO and similar bodies were officially nonpolitical, cultural organizations) to claims of intellectual standing based on political representation. This also affected nonpolitical international scientific societies. They are under constant pressure—to which all have succumbed to various degrees—to elect officers and to invite participants to conferences on the basis of national representation. This politicization of international science has considerably weakened the informal but highly effective mechanisms of the international scientific community which—for the last three hundred years—upheld and spread universalistic standards throughout the world. As a result, the strategy of claiming international recognition for poor local scholarship on nationalist grounds has become much more effective than ever before.

GROUP
MOBILITY
THROUGH
HIGHER
EDUCATION IN
DEVELOPED
COUNTRIES

These developments on the international scene have been paralleled by the previously mentioned shift in the interpretation of the meaning of "equal opportunity" from equal chance to equal share. According to this view, in principle any group capable of defining itself politically and whose members are less than proportionately represented among students or teachers in higher education could press for a publicly enforced quota for its members. In fact, such a quota system has been instituted in the United States for blacks, Latinos, women, and Asians, but these last have turned out to be overrepresented (in principle, quotas also apply to native Americans, but their numbers are too small to have recognizable effect).

Quota systems have also been in force in such multiethnic countries as the U.S.S.R. and Canada, but their systems are based on ethnic segregation. Soviet republics and Canadian provinces have distinct national characteristics, so that the problem in those countries is more similar to that of separate nations. The relationship of the Russian to the other Soviet republics is that of center to periphery. The Canadian case is more complicated, since there the dominant English provinces are not the cultural center for the French province of Quebec. Still, these are clear-cut national problems. The only precedent to group quotas have been the quotas favoring working-class youth in university admissions that have been in force in all Communist countries for decades.[5] No other country has a quota system, but in all there is a tendency to monitor the performance of higher educational systems in terms of class or ethnic representation.

It is not known what induced this change in interpretation of social justice in higher education. It is possible that the change was related to the view of research and knowledge as productive resources. This view—which became the ruling dogma in science and higher educational policy in the 1950s and early 1960s—could lead to demands for equal shares. If research, namely, the creation of new knowledge, is a productive

---

[5]Quota systems were also in force in several European countries between the two world wars. Unlike the present ones, meant to increase the "representation" of minorities, those in the 1920s and 1930s were intended to reduce the fraction of students belonging to minorities—especially Jews—in higher education.

resource, then the study of that knowledge confers on the student a share in that resource. Educational equality is thus often perceived today as analogous to land distribution between peasants.

Of course, land distribution does not help the peasants unless they know how to grow crops. But at least if they do know, they may eat their own produce. In higher education this is not possible. A lawyer who has no clients cannot feed on his or her briefs. Hence extending professional higher education beyond the demand for labor is bound to lead to the unemployment, underemployment, and frustration that were endemic to the academically trained groups in continental Europe between the two world wars, and in some European countries even earlier.

These considerations were known and acted upon before the Second World War in Britain and the United States, so that these two countries were relatively immune to intellectual unemployment (Ben-David, 1963–64; Kotschnig, 1937). But the research euphoria of the late 1950s and early 1960s and the large government subsidies for research and higher education changed this situation. Partly as a result of these inducements, and partly as a result of the widely held belief that education was a productive resource, British and American universities grossly overestimated their effectiveness as mechanisms of social placement. Abandoning their traditional caution, they began acting on the assumption that there was an unlimited demand for higher education, which was no longer seen as merely one of the channels through which one moved into a social position, but as a promise of obtaining such a position. Learning was seen as an endless frontier with homesteads enough for all. Universities appeared to be one of the main sources of economic and, in a way, political power. Myths circulated about Route 128 in Boston, where science-based industries spawned by MIT and Harvard turned knowledge into new products, high incomes, and a new way of life. There were tales of the new science town of Novosibirsk in the U.S.S.R. and dreams of towns like that everywhere.

This created a dangerous situation for the universities. As long as university diplomas were regarded only as tickets to lucrative jobs, the frustration of hopes of social ascent through education was blamed on a society that did not provide the jobs, rather than on the university. When the university was perceived as an economic and political institution of central importance, playing an important role in the creation and allocation of jobs, it became not only the source but also the target of class envy and violence. If the university was an important source of wealth and power, then the capture and domination of the university was an important part of the struggle for social advantage.

All this made the status of the academics invidious. As long as people believed that science would solve the problems of mankind within a reasonably short time, there were no overt manifestations of status envy. People might have been jealous of the newly gained status of scientists, but they suppressed their jealousy because they had respect for science. But once disappointment with science set in, the university began to appear as a source of privilege and power, and it became an easy target of attacks and demands for redistribution by political radicals.

This set the background for the introduction of the idea of equal shares in higher education to politically defined groups in linguistically and nationally homogeneous societies. Although this is the same idea as that of establishing educational equality among nations, two important elements of that idea—namely, separate languages and territories—are missing in the demands for equal shares for different groups within a single nation.

This is an important difference. Demands for the recognition of the languages and cultures of peripheral or dominated peoples as legitimate vehicles and objects of academic study could be—in principle—justified by generally acceptable universalistic terms. The educational status of cultural groups was expected to improve through individuals taking advantage of the new opportunity to study in their own language and in their own country (even if in practice this expectation was not always realized—see above, p. 152). And the scholarly study of a culture previously not studied by scientific methods was a contribution to universal learning.

Another justification of educational independence for national groups has been territorial. Cultural peripheries dependent on metropoles may get less than their share of educational and professional services, because their intellectual elites gravitate toward the center. The establishment of national universities and other independent cultural institutions in peripheral countries may be a means to counteract this tendency.

Demands for educational equality between linguistically homogeneous social groups—on other than a territorial basis—lack these justifications. Instead, they are justified in two other ways. One is the suspicion that the practices of universities and other academic institutions may not measure up to their universalistic standards and may be actually discriminatory. Therefore, many people are willing to try group quotas in education because they feel that these might help to eliminate unseen barriers and prejudices and eventually give rise to better, more universalistic standards. Others have concluded that there are no universalistic standards in higher education, and that standards of science and scholarship are merely reflections of the cultural biases of the white, male, middle-class groups that created them. They therefore consider educational advancement as a political distribution of privileges.

Because of these considerations, the idea that the status of different groups—as distinct from different cultures—must be equalized through higher educational quotas has become widely accepted, especially in the United States. So-called affirmative action programs require that universities ensure "proper representation" of different minority groups and women at universities as students, graduates, and staff. But, as has been pointed out, the idea is by no means confined to the United States.

EFFECTS OF POLITICALLY ENFORCED EDUCATIONAL EQUALIZATION The widespread acceptance of enforced equalization in education is new, and its effects are impossible to foretell, but, although the idea—as explicitly formulated today—is new, the practice is not, so that its effects are known. As has been pointed out, the assertion of cultural independence has—in some cases—benefited only the local intellectuals without either benefiting the national culture or facilitating the educational mobility of individuals. The results of this assertion have also been disappointing in multinational countries, such as the U.S.S.R. and Canada, in which quota systems have been applied to create educational equality between the constituting nationalities. Differences in educational attainment have persisted, and there is no evidence that the educational attainment of the different ethnic groups would have been lower if, instead of quotas and other group measures, efforts had been concentrated on improvement of educational facilities and teaching among disadvantaged groups. Therefore, one must conclude that, as means of achieving rapid educational breakthroughs, group quotas are likely to have disappointing results.

As for the more extreme philosophical claim that symbolic equalization of different nations and ethnic groups is a necessary condition for the elimination of the cultural domination of Western "middle-class" science and scholarship and for its replacement with a more variegated scene of many advanced cultures, the existing evidence is unequivocally negative. The development of none of the new national or ethnic systems of higher education created since the early nineteenth century supports the assertion that modern science and scholarship reflect purely Western cultural biases. Nowhere has a new type of science arisen, or a new type of scholarship, other than the prevailing, so-called Western one. There are great differences in the quality of higher education and research in different nations, but no basic differences in content, methods, or epistemological assumptions. There are said to be some differences in national styles of research, but no one is sure what they are, and all the countries that have been mentioned in this respect have adopted "Western" science and scholarship. Nor has the more than 50-year-old attempt to create a new "proletarian" culture in the U.S.S.R. led to the emergence of a science and scholarship (or, for that matter, art) based on assumptions different from the so-called Western bourgeois science and scholarship (or art).

Therefore it is impossible to justify quotas on educational or cultural grounds. Perhaps they can be useful as political means to buy the goodwill of certain groups by apportioning to them parts of higher education, and to aid their absorption into the American social and political systems. This is a question that does not properly belong here. But it has to be made clear that if quotas will not eliminate educational inequality, they are unlikely to create political goodwill either. In fact, by arousing expectations that may be frustrated, their effect may be the opposite. But even if the attempt to create political goodwill succeeds, it may still be harmful to the universities in the long run. It would confirm the effectiveness of the universities as political institutions and encourage their use for political purposes. This would probably lead to their intellectual decline, as the political success of medieval universities led to their decline in the late Middle Ages.

Paradoxically, this would also diminish their limited use as a mechanism of social equalization. Individual merit may be unequally distributed among classes, but a system based upon it still creates a great deal of mobility, especially if science and learning are free to grow and diversify. But a system of higher education used by politically powerful groups to consolidate their positions may easily become a source of ascribed privilege.

CONCLUSION Higher education appears to have been primarily a channel of individual mobility. It has also upgraded the status of some occupations and created new ones, increasing thereby the size of the middle and upper-middle classes. Since its value as a mechanism of social placement derives from the fact that educational success distinguishes the competent from the incompetent, the potential of higher education as a means of creating greater equality is limited. It can provide equal opportunities to all, and it may be able to help the disadvantaged to overcome inherited educational disabilities. But it cannot ensure the equal distribution of educational success among classes or other politically active groups.

Nevertheless, higher education has been used to create equality of status between different national and ethnic groups for a longer time and in more diverse contexts than is usually realized. Its effectiveness in this respect has been limited, and the results of such attempts have been, in many cases, purely symbolic or even negative. National or ethnic institutions of higher education—whatever their symbolic value for the group—may lead to the emergence and the strengthening of the position of politically defined groups of intellectuals lacking professional competence. The entrenchment of such groups in the system of higher education reduces its effectiveness in every respect and will also reduce its contribution to the educational advancement of the group in general and of the able students within the group in particular.

Higher education can make a real contribution to social justice only by effectively educating properly prepared, able, and motivated individuals from all classes and groups. Therefore, the shift in the meaning of educational equality from individual to representative group mobility has had a harmful effect. Further growth toward educational equality is—as has been seen—still possible, but only if there will be technical advance in educational methods, and if expenditures will be increased. The politicization of the issue has tended to divert attention from potentially effective measures.

8. Higher Education Today: Problems and Challenges

In summarizing the implications of the preceding analyses for the state of higher education today, it will be useful to look at some of the indexes of growth since the 1940s. Developments toward what is sometimes called mass higher education began in the United States in the 1920s.[1] All other countries have entered this stage of development since the 1950s. By 1929–30, 12 percent of youth aged 18 to 21 were enrolled in colleges in the United States (Harris, 1972, pp. 412–413), but in no other country was the percentage higher than 10 before 1950 (the typical percentage was 3 to 4). Since the 1960s the percentages have exceeded 10 in all the developed countries; in some of them they are higher than 20; and in the United States the percentage is higher than 40 (Harris, 1972, p. 435). Another way of looking at the change is to relate student enrollments to the general population: In 1950 only one country, the United States, enrolled more than 1,000 students (more exactly, 1,508) per 100,000 inhabitants, and most countries enrolled fewer than 500; in 1966 there was no industrially advanced country with an enrollment of less than 1,000 students per 100,000 inhabitants (in the United States the ratio was 3,425 per 100,000) (Harris, 1972, p. 433).

As has been seen, this means that higher education all over the world has assumed new functions. Two of these, namely, active furtherance of the professionalization of the occupational structure through the institution of degree courses in an

---

[1] As a term describing the state of higher education in the United States, "mass higher education" is misleading in that it implies a leveling of standards and absence of differentiation, whereas exactly the opposite is true. But the term has been accepted and used in the literature. For an authoritative discussion of the transition to mass higher education, see Trow (1973).

increasing variety of occupations, and the education of a considerable number of "general" students who do not study for
any definite profession (at least for their first degree), were
well-established university functions in the United States after
the 1920s, and perhaps even earlier. But elsewhere (with the
partial exception of the U.S.S.R.) the situation was different.
Professions were few and there was great reluctance to extend
professional privilege. Before the war in England and Germany
professional status was rigidly tied to certain traditionally recognized disciplines and fields, and, in England, also to the social
standing of the professional organizations. French conceptions
of occupations requiring academic training emphasized types
of erudition rather than disciplinary study and research, but
were also restricted by tradition. Today this has changed.
Professional status is accorded to an increasing variety of voca-
tions, and there is, on the whole, no greater reluctance in
Europe to extend professional status to new research-based
occupations than in the United States. Professional training is
now training in any vocation that has a basis in research,
including such areas as education or social work in which this
research is not firmly rooted in recognized scientific disciplines.

The change in the education of the general student has been
equally conspicuous. Those who went to universities in Europe
in the 1920s and 1930s studied in order to become higher civil
servants, lawyers, physicians, pharmacists, engineers, industrial chemists, high school teachers, economists, academics,
and members of a few smaller professions. Higher education
was in balance when the number of graduates corresponded to
the demand for such professionals. When it exceeded
demand—which it frequently did—graduates became unemployable and alienated from society. The absolute numbers of
the unemployable graduates were not large, but the graduates
were concentrated in the capital cities, and because they were
articulate and well connected, their political and cultural influence was disproportionately great. Governments made great,
and usually unsuccessful, efforts to solve the problem of unem-
ployed intellectuals. But in spite of repeated failures, it was
taken for granted that the solution to the problem was to
establish and maintain a balance between the supply of graduates and the demand for professional workers (Kotschnig,
1937).

With 15 percent or more of the college-age group studying at universities, the possibility of establishing such balance has vanished. Whether they like it or not, universities are now training a large number of students who will have no chance of becoming professional workers, even in the extended sense of this term as used in this book (see Chapter 3). Thus the education of what has been called in this book the general student has become since the 1940s one of the permanent functions of higher education in Europe (and in many places outside Europe), as it has been a function of American higher education since the end of the last century (Ushiogi, 1971).[2]

A third function, the professionalization and large-scale development of university research, has been, to a large extent, new even in the United States (although less so than elsewhere). There were professional research workers and some organized research in the universities before the Second World War, but its extent was insignificant (see Table 3 in Chapter 5). Now research accompanies everyday life. It consumes 2 to 3 per cent of the GNP and is an integral part of the everyday routine of agriculture, medicine, many branches of manufacturing, education, social welfare, and economic policy making.

There are no indications that any of these trends are going to be reversed. In spite of a slowdown in enrollments in most places due to demographic factors, demand for higher education among the middle and upper classes has not significantly declined, and one can expect that the drive to raise the chances of entry of lower-class youth will continue. Further enrollment increases can be expected from equalizing women's chances of entry with those of men. These two conditions should assure a further increase in the fraction of the college-age group attending university or college in almost every country.[3] Of course, absolute numbers depend on the birthrate and economic conditions, but there is no indication of any basic change in the public taste for higher education.

Demand in the labor market for people with university

---

[2] According to Morikazu Ushiogi (1976, pp. 4–5), the ratio of professional workers among university graduates drops significantly when the number of graduates exceeds 5 percent of the age group.

[3] These considerations are based on a report by the Carnegie Commission on Higher Education (1971, p. 2). The report predicts for the United States an enrollment rate of about 50 percent of the age group by 2000.

degrees is also more likely to increase than to decrease—at least outside the United States. The reason for this is that university graduates everywhere compete with others for jobs that do not necessarily require university training, such as public administration, business, or banking. Past experience shows that once this process of professionalization begins, the possession of a degree or a diploma sooner or later becomes a necessary qualification of entry into such jobs (Ushiogi, 1971).

It is also difficult to expect a significant drop in the overall demand for research. The habit of relying on research for the solution of all kinds of problems is stronger and more widespread today than ever before, and the awareness of problems requiring solution has not diminished (Boffey, 1976). Thus, as far as external demand is concerned, long-term prospects for higher education are not unfavorable.

But, as has been seen throughout this book, there are serious questions about the ability of universities to muster the internal resources needed to perform their functions in general education and research. According to the conclusions of the previous chapters, it seems that only one function—professional education—presents no difficulty. Although not all higher education systems provide effective professional training for all or most of their students, they all provide opportunities for the acquisition of professional knowledge and skills, at least for the more energetic students. And they have all come to accept the possibility of extending from time to time the range of professional occupations. The changes that have occurred in professional education since the 1940s have not created problems unencountered in the past, and by and large existing structures have been able to handle the changes reasonably well.

This has not been true for the performance of the other university functions. The continental European system is ill-adapted to deal with the general student who has no definite vocational or intellectual purpose, but who comes to the university to enlarge his or her horizon and to develop an intellectual and moral identity. American and British universities are better adapted to this task, but even in these countries universities have become less effective than they were in the past.

There are equally serious difficulties with university research. All systems have always been engaged in research, but the changes that have occurred since the 1940s have been fundamental: Graduate education and university research have become a semi-industrialized professional enterprise within the American university and their links with liberal education have weakened. Elsewhere, efforts were made to follow the American example of developing graduate education and organized research in the universities. Since, however, these efforts coincided with rapid increases in undergraduate admissions and were not accompanied by appropriate changes in the university structure or an adequate increase in financing the absorption of the students, integration of research with teaching became an even more difficult problem than in the United States. The situation has worsened during the last few years. As long as demand for research was brisk and universities benefited from research financially, there was some compensation for the difficulties of integrating research with the other functions. Now with the decline of demand, research has become a financial drag on universities, so that this compensation has gone.

In addition to these difficulties in coping with their extended functions of general education and research, universities have been under pressure for direct involvement in politics, and for serving as a channel of mobility for politically defined groups. These pressures have been an indirect result of the newly extended functions of the universities. Sheer numerical growth has increased the likelihood of their political involvement, and the concomitant growth of their importance as a mechanism of occupational placement has directed increased political attention to the possibility of using them as a device to create social equality. However, as has been pointed out, universities can contribute to such broad political ends only in a manner consistent with good teaching and research, namely through disciplined thinking about such problems, and strict adherence to universalistic standards in admissions, teaching, and research. They have to resist pressures for more direct and comprehensive political involvement, and to try and regain social support and rehabilitate their internal morale through overcoming their difficulties in teaching and research.

Suggestions for Reform

Differentiation of functions in continental Europe

According to the present analysis, the problems of the continental European systems are different from those of the American and British systems. The former systems have not recognized that the university has general educational functions.

With only slight exaggeration one can say that in spite of the differences between them, French and German universities today are attended by large numbers of general students, are staffed by faculties that think of themselves as teachers in graduate schools of arts and sciences, and confer degrees supposedly certifying professional qualification.

The reason for the resistance to differentiating the functions of the universities and to complementing them with degree-granting institutions of a different kind seems to be that the continental European universities have preserved some of the traditional privileges of a respected medieval estate. Professors have few formal duties and are accountable to no one, except in a very vague and ineffective way to their peers. Students also enjoy traditional freedoms, such as a very lax regimen of studies; political privileges, symbolized by the exterritoriality of the university to the police, and the toleration of student delinquencies by the authorities as "youthful excesses"; and a prestigeful social status. This latter is temporary, but—since the expense of studying is usually negligible, and sometimes even negative because of generous stipends, subsidized meals and housing, and the like—it is easily acquired and extended far beyond the number of years needed to prepare for the degree.[4] This freedom can be legitimated only to the extent that universities as a whole are considered seats of advanced research and study. Teachers and students engaged in such work do not, indeed, require much educational guidance and direction and can be relied on to structure their work autonomously.

This combination of advanced research and study has been realized only in small parts of the university, but those parts, in which teachers and students use their freedom for its original purpose of research and study, have legitimated the turning of freedom by others who do no research or study into unjustified privilege. As a result, the idea of the free research university, which is supposed to unify research and teaching at all levels, has been maintained in the new mass university under circumstances that do not always justify it. In fact, the idea has now been officially adopted also in France, where it was not quite accepted until recently. Thus the units of the French university

---

[4] The attempts of some European governments to curtail the privileges of those prolonging studies is resisted by students and many teachers as a reactionary act of anti-intellectualism.

system, according to the 1968 reforms, are called "units of teaching and research" (*unités d'enseignement et recherche*, or U.E.R.). Paradoxically, the attempt to cope with the problems of students dissatisfied with the traditional disciplinary framework of instruction is based on the very idea—the unity of research and teaching—that gave rise to the disciplinary framework. Making research-based instruction more suitable for the general student by creating interdisciplinary units was based on a misconception of all research, disciplinary and interdisciplinary. Both require specialized technical knowledge, the latter usually more than the former. The attempt shows an almost irrational adherence to the mystique of a free community of teachers and students engaged in research. As has been pointed out, such a community is to a degree possible on the graduate level. But to believe that such a community could be created from (often ill-prepared) general students and from teachers—some of whom are also ill-prepared for research—is pure self-deception.

Attempts are now being made, particularly in Germany, to overcome the resistance to differentiation. There are experiments in combining universities, teacher-training colleges, engineering schools, and schools for technicians into a single comprehensive institution of higher education (the *Gesamthochschule*), and there is new legislation to regulate teaching careers in all kinds of postsecondary education. And some countries (for example, France, Japan, Yugoslavia) have made attempts to divide postsecondary education into three levels, according to the American pattern. It is impossible to foretell the results of these attempts. But one has the impression that so far these experiments have not properly taken account of the function of general education. They confer some academic standing to certain types of technical-vocational education, but the idea that universities have to provide a meaningful and intellectually challenging education for general students—some who may be very able but who do not have a specific professional purpose—has still not been accepted in these countries. First-level general educational courses—where they exist—are not being conducted on an academic level; they have little prestige; and their relation to higher-level studies is ill defined. They are considered as a peripheral part of the university, like the technical-vocational courses.

But the introduction of vocational courses into the university is an entirely different problem from that of general education. The former can be insulated from the rest of the university. As long as they train their students well, they perform a useful function even if their standards are academically unsatisfactory. In any event they will have little impact on the university as a whole.

General education cannot be insulated from the rest of the university. It has to provide a taste and an idea of advanced study, and—for those interested and able to continue—it has to provide the experience and knowledge required for an intelligent choice of specialized study. Furthermore, since these courses are designed for the large bulk of students and are usually a prerequisite for graduate-level studies, they will be a source of widespread frustration among both students and teachers if they are not done well. Thus proper organization of and adequate resources for these studies are a necessary condition of the effective functioning of all present-day systems of higher education. The reasons for the reluctance to recognize this problem in the continental European universities have been explained above (Chapter 4). They have neither the academic organization—like the collegial structure of Oxford and Cambridge, or the deans and masters of American colleges— required to maintain such a multidisciplinary enterprise, nor the tradition of excellence in liberal education prevailing in leading American and British institutions.

It is true that even in these latter countries the growth of research enterprise in the 1950s and 1960s weakened the incentive of teachers to devote their time to the education of undergraduates as well as the interests of students to obtain a good liberal education. Increasingly undergraduate studies came to be regarded as mere preliminaries to the graduate course. But these developments were the result of market conditions temporarily favoring research. Now that those conditions have changed, interest in the education of the general student has revived. In any event, the vitality of general higher education has been maintained in these countries. There have always been institutions in which the fraction of highly qualified undergraduates interested in a high-level and not-too-specialized education has been large enough to make undergraduate teaching an intellectually rewarding experience for outstanding teachers, including quite a few who are also outstanding in research. Therefore, even though liberal education is of very poor quality in many American colleges and is virtually nonexistent in many British universities, the institutional framework necessary to improve the situation is available in these countries. But in continental Europe, or even Japan, there are still neither institutional frameworks nor incentives for either students or teachers to seek excellence in general education.[5] With general students becoming an increasingly greater fraction of the student body, the inability to advance these studies to a plane on which they can be considered as really higher education may lead to a general leveling down of the standards of the universities and to the eventual transfer of advanced research into nonuniversity research institutes.

POLITICAL AND MORAL EDUCATION The reluctance to deal with the intellectual aspect of general higher education is a problem mainly in continental Europe, but the refusal to provide moral guidance to students is common to all nontotalitarian systems. There are good reasons for this: Norms of moral conduct are controversial, and university instructors are not chosen for their ability to provide moral leadership.

In spite of all this, there are overwhelming arguments in favor of moral education: namely, many students are in need of such education, and there is a minimum degree of morality without which no institution can survive. What has actually happened at universities is that students in search of a moral identity try to find it where they can.

Since the university as an institution and its formal curriculum insist on the principle of value neutrality, such students must find moral guidance among those who do not respect this principle, namely, in radical circles. These offer a cause to which one can commit oneself, and a group to identify with. Their ideologies pretend to be scientific, and at the same time they offer "solutions" to all the problems of the individual and

[5] Raising the status of the teacher in general education by conferring high salary and titles, as is now done in Germany, Britain, and elsewhere for teachers in nonconventional types of higher education, will probably discourage excellence. Since the group is promoted as a category, and not on the basis of differential attainment, they will be inclined to "routinize" their work and to promote their interests through collective bargaining rather than outstanding service.

the world. Thus the policy that universities must not take any stand on political and moral issues—a policy considered an essential condition of preserving the objectivity of science and the autonomy of universities—has led to diametrically opposed results. The policy has been observed only by those respecting the autonomy of science, and not by others; those opposed to the autonomy of science feel free to try to politicize the universities, while those in favor of autonomy refrain from defending their position because such defense would be a political act. Thus, many university departments insisting on the value neutrality of science have become centers of ideological indoctrination and revolutionary cells in recent years (and, in Europe, also in the past).

The question is what can be done about this. Science cannot fight back with the same methods as its opponents and pretend to offer salvation and moral certitude. But it can certainly do more than it has been doing lately.

Part of the problem seems to be a misinterpretation of the principle of value neutrality. As usually interpreted, this principle has two meanings: that scientific judgment has to be free from emotional involvement, based on universally valid standards of evidence, and uninfluenced by extraneous interests, and that one cannot derive moral judgments from scientific statements. Neither of these interpretations is entirely correct. The norms of scientific judgment do not imply that the scientist is not motivated by certain values. The very adoption of these norms implies that the pursuit of truth is a value; otherwise the norms would make no sense. Actually, scientific judgment is not dispassionate. It is inspired by the passion to find the truth. A scientist capable of overcoming his or her financial interests or ethnic prejudices in accepting or rejecting a theory is no more detached than a person who is impelled to act against these same interests or prejudices by passionate love for a woman or a man. The impossibility of deriving moral judgments from scientific statements is also not quite valid. There is a relationship between factual and moral statements. Thus, the statement that a theorem is proven, or that the results of a crucial experiment contradict one and support the other of two hypotheses, implies an obligation to accept the proven theorem or the supported hypothesis. Therefore, universities stand for definite values. The principle of value neutrality does not mean an absence of values, but the subjection of other values to that of the scientific search for truth. And the results of scientific research impose an obligation to reject and accept ideas publicly with all the implications of such rejection and acceptance. Unambiguous identification of the university with these values and insistence on norms of speech and conduct consistent with them would in itself go some way toward filling the moral void felt at universities.

But the problem of moral education is not only a lack of attention to the values of science. Students in search of moral education would like the university to provide them with a comprehensive, intellectually coherent, and existentially meaningful outlook. This, of course, cannot be provided by science or scholarship, and the reluctance of universities to adopt a social or political outlook is understandable. Any commitment of this kind is a potential threat to scientific value neutrality. But the fact is, many students are not adults and need moral guidance while studying at the university; this fact cannot be disregarded.

One possibility in dealing with the problem would be—as has been suggested—to involve the university much more actively and on a much higher level in the moral and political self-education of students. But perhaps one might consider also the more radical measure of creating universities openly committed to a religious or sociopolitical outlook. In the not-so-distant past—actually until the 1950s—leading American and English universities often had a pronounced religious and philosophical outlook. They were politically liberal (in the classical eighteenth- and nineteenth-century sense) and espoused a tolerant kind of Christianity and an ideal of gentlemanly behavior and way of life. This commitment was abandoned during the 1950s. During those years there was a far-reaching consensus in the free democracies about political and moral outlook, so that people lost interest in the subject. What more or less everyone took for granted was not worth talking about, and those who did were usually bores. Furthermore, as has been pointed out, there were always abuses due to the adoption of this or that outlook—such as discrimination against competent teachers and students on religious or social grounds—and a hypocritical endorsement of norms and rules that were respected by only a few. Therefore, American and British academics were as happy to opt for a morally neutral university in the 1950s as their continental European counterparts had been many years before.

It is likely, however, that the abuses could have been corrected without extinguishing, or, rather, driving underground, all concern with moral outlook. In any case, the policy of moral neutrality has been unsuccessful, and perhaps the time has come for new experiments. It is not easy to say what forms these should take. The main question is to what extent academic institutions as a whole can commit themselves to a certain outlook. The experience of denominational schools in the United States and of socialist institutions of higher education in Germany and Denmark is not very encouraging. The denominational universities have failed because they represent relatively fundamentalist religious positions that mean little to the majority of students and teachers and that are in many respects inconsistent with a scientific outlook. To overcome the resulting apathy or hostility toward religious values, such institutions make attempts to adopt fashionable political or social ideologies and pretend that these ideologies are related to the religious values of the institution. Since, as a matter of fact, there is no such relationship, the result is that the ideological fashions are adopted, but the religious values lose even more ground than before. The problem with the socialist experiments is that they apparently do not respect academic freedom and that they exercise gross discrimination against nonsocialists. Thus they cannot be regarded as experiments in scientific higher education.

The evidence, therefore, on whether universities committed to a religious or sociopolitical outlook could succeed is not clear. Perhaps the very absence of serious experiments shows that few teachers or students interested in higher education are committed to a definite outlook. However, the relative success of the committed British and American universities of the past, and the long-standing failure of the uncommitted universities in continental Europe to stem hooliganism, indicate that renewed experiments with universities committed to an outlook may be justified, provided that the outlook would be explicitly consistent with the values of science and that these would be better safeguards than in the past against discrimination, prejudice, and hypocrisy.

In any event, whether there will emerge institutions committed to a definite outlook, or whether institutions will prefer to abstain from such commitment, no institution can afford to continue justifying moral irresponsibility by misinterpreted scientific value neutrality. Universities will have to make clear that they stand for the values of science, and they will have to adopt institutional policies toward the moral education of students. A modern university can and probably should be an institution pluralistic in the outlooks of its members, and it has to be a critical institution, since criticism is part of the core of science. But it cannot be a morally cynical institution, as it very nearly became in the 1960s.

Devoting serious attention to the problem of moral education at the universities may not only help students and the universities, but also society. One of the worst ills of the democratic societies of the 1970s is moral disillusionment and absence of leadership. One of the causes of this development may be that the universities—which have obtained an almost complete monopoly of educating everybody destined for an important career in politics or any other walk of life—have virtually declared a taboo on moral education. At the only place where young people could seriously come to grips with problems of right and wrong as they appear in the particular context of their generation, moral concerns are virtually driven underground, surfacing only in the deformations of totalitarian sects in which force and violence substitute for intellectual conviction and moral commitment. Universities cannot content themselves by simply declaring that this is none of their concern.

RECONCEPTUALIZATION OF UNIVERSITY RESEARCH Next to general education, the university function that requires most adaptation to changed circumstances is research. University research has to settle down to a realistic rate of growth that does not greatly exceed that of the economy over periods of many years. In Britain and the United States it has to reestablish its links with general and professional education. In continental Europe the problem is more difficult, because if present trends continue, there is a question whether research will have a place in the universities at all.

Much of the problem everywhere is economic. But the roots of the present economic stringency in research go back to misconceptions that emerged in the 1960s about the nature of scientific growth and about the economic utility of research. The main indication of these misconceptions was the virtual abandonment of the term *pure research* to describe science serving no purpose other than the discovery of truth and its replacement with the term *basic* or *fundamental* research. The implication of this change of terms was that even if the scientist's motives were "purely" intellectual, his or her work was fundamental to work of a more applied character. The sources of this view were some macroeconomic studies that indicated that in the United States returns on investment in the production and diffusion of knowledge were high. The studies were no more than a first approach to the problem, and their general applicability was questionable. But the idea was popularized and—combined with slogans taken from sociological literature, such as "postindustrial" or "knowledge" society—led to the emergence of a scientific utopia. The relationship between research, knowledge, and the economy was conceived as a kind of *perpetuum mobile*. In this utopia, capital, land, and labor lost their importance, and the economic future seemed to depend mainly on scientific and technological knowledge. Because that knowledge was believed to grow at an exponential rate, providing enough resources for research and improving the diffusion of knowledge were considered some of the most important conditions of economic growth. Governments were urged to regard the expansion of higher education and investment in research as an important part of their economic policy (Price, 1963, p. 111). Since Western economies were reasonably healthy at that time, they could afford to pay attention to and even act on these recommendations.

This gave rise to the practice of supporting—in principle— every research project deemed to be competent by panels of experts, or, in other words, the previously mentioned (see Chapter 5) turning of the peer-review system into a policy-making mechanism. All, including "basic" science, was supported on economic grounds as a productive resource, with the result that graduate departments and university research institutes were regarded as productive units, rather than integral parts of the educational and training operations of the university.

All these ideas on the economic significance of research and the possibility of force-feeding the growth of knowledge through investment were exaggerated. Research has been a good investment only under certain conditions, and it became rapidly evident that the recommendations for investing as much as possible in research as a basis for economic development did not take into account that in the production of knowledge—as in everything else—there are diminishing returns (Weinberg, 1967, pp. 156–160).[6]

It was also entirely unjustified to expect that the investment itself could create knowledge. Money does not make discoveries; only a very small fraction of people do. They, too, can make them only when the "time is ripe": namely, when the information and tools necessary for the solution of a problem are available, when these tools have been or can be assembled by potential discoverers through education and training, and when the attention of potential discoverers is not detracted to insignificant problems by fruitless scientific traditions or fashions. Money can be of decisive importance if there is an unused capacity of potential discoverers when the time is ripe. It is also likely that money can help to extend the number of potential discoverers, and that the new discoveries made as a result of increased investment will accelerate the "ripening of time." But both these effects are probably subject to rapidly diminishing returns. The long history of independent multiple discoveries, and the widespread anticipation of the research results of one scientist by others even today, when one can easily find out what every scientist in one's field is working on, suggest that problems for which the time is ripe are always scarce (Hagstrom, 1965, p. 75; Merton, 1973, pp. 343–370). Moreover, investigations of scientific citations show that increasing scientific production does not produce a proportionate increase in the production of knowledge actually used (quoted) by scientists, probably because the knowledge thus produced is less significant (Cole & Cole, 1973, pp. 216–234; Price, 1963, pp. 53–54, 73–82). All this suggests fairly narrow limits within which the

[6] There are no quantitative comparative studies of returns to investment in research proper. But to the extent one can extrapolate findings of research on investment in education (acquisition of knowledge) to investment in research (creation of knowledge), they support this statement on diminishing returns. Thus while in the less-developed countries "the average return to investment in education (19.9 per cent) is higher than the average return to physical capital (15.1 per cent), the opposite seems to be the case in advanced countries (returns of 8.3 and 10.5 per cent, respectively)" (Psacharopoulos, 1973, p. 8).

production of original "basic" knowledge can be stimulated by investment.

Thus the concept of university research as being part of a system of organized—one may almost say "industrial"—production of economically useful knowledge is untenable. Not all research is economically useful, and the attempt to obliterate the difference between that which is and that which is not has—in the long run—only harmed science.

Support for the two kinds of science has to be based on distinct criteria. Research that is to be applied has to be demonstrably applicable and has to be judged applicable by its actual users, who are usually nonscientists. Support of such research has to be justified by more than macroeconomic calculations of global returns; there has to be a clear connection between research and the solution of the problem for which it has been undertaken. On the other hand, the need to train researchers—applied and other—and to train college and university teachers in the education of students interested in the intellectual adventure of original discovery requires pure research in which the investigator decides autonomously what to investigate and submits his or her findings to the judgment of peers. Support of such research cannot be based on possible benefits to the economy as a whole or to the solution of a practical problem, since the purpose of such research is to solve intellectual problems that arise in the course of study and research irrespective of whether these are undertaken out of the purely cognitive need to understand physical or human nature or out of a variety of economic or other personal motives.

These are, of course, not readily applicable criteria to determine the amount of support to be given for university research. But they suggest the mechanisms required for obtaining and distributing support. Universities have to reorient themselves from supplying an internal market whose graduates are reabsorbed in university research, working on problems of interest to the ever-expanding scientific community, to serving external markets. They have to show enterprise in finding clients and flexibility in serving them through research and training. This need not lead to any lowering of standards. Some of the most outstanding institutes of technology in the world, especially in the industrially advanced small European countries—such as those in Zurich, Delft, Stockholm, or Trondheim—have always trained their students for industry, employed as professors people with industrial practice, and engaged in a great deal of industrial research (Organisation for Economic Co-operation and Development, 1973, pp. 137–142). This, of course, also used to be the case in American institutes of technology until the 1950s, when the tide turned and institutes went out of their way to become as far as possible like schools of basic science. This latter trend is now being reversed, and universities are making efforts to orient their work to more applied and practical kinds of training and research.

Actually this is not so much reorientation to more practical kinds of research, but a renewed search for new areas for the application of research. In the 1950s a number of then new areas in space research, computer technology, and the like emerged. Originally, research in these was also of a much cruder kind than that in universities and rarely required a Ph.D. degree. Eventually, because of the growth of these industries and generous support from governments, work in these fields became of academic level. Because of the interlocking relationship among universities, industry, and government—with the last-named supplying most of the money—research grew far beyond the point of economic or even technological usefulness, although ostensibly all this was applied or, at least, mission-oriented basic research. This led to inevitable cutbacks, accelerated, but not caused, by general economic difficulties. Probably much of the disappointment with this research was actually due to its having reached an impasse, rather than to any ideological conviction, in which much disillusionment was couched in the heady days of the late 1960s.[7]

Such reorientation from overdeveloped to underdeveloped fields of application will probably yield not only practically but also theoretically useful results, since any application of science to the solution of new problems is likely to create new theoretical insights. Thus, it will also benefit pure science. Of course, such indirect benefits cannot constitute a sufficient basis for the support of pure science. New insights, whether derived from practical work or generated by theoretically oriented research, need funds and other resources to be developed. Therefore, in

---

[7] For an interesting account of the reorientation from mainly defense-sponsored to a greater variety of mission-oriented research in the Fluid Mechanics Laboratory of the Mechanical Engineering Department at MIT, see Probstein (1970).

addition to support for applied work, there have to be mechanisms for the support of pure research.

These mechanisms have to perform two functions: one is the routine task of providing sufficient funds for the research required for graduate-level training. Since universities will increasingly have to train students—including Ph.D.'s—for a variety of tasks outside the university, the number of advanced students will be a good basis for estimating the socially needed size of graduate training operations. Assuming that all those who train students on advanced levels have to be actively engaged in research, this estimate can also serve as a starting point to assess the need for research routinely required for educational purposes in a system.

Of course, it can be argued that advanced students can be trained as well through applied as through pure research, and there is a strong tendency today to accept this argument. Evidently, there is no particular advantage in research that cannot be applied to anything, and "purity" in research is not an end in itself. But the definition of pure science used here does not imply any preference for "purity" for its own sake. Such research can be of immediate practical value and may be actually motivated by practical interest. All that is recommended here is that investigators be free to decide which problems to investigate and that they be judged primarily on the basis of the intrinsic intellectual value of their contribution by peers competent to make such judgment.[8] Since the function of this research is to order and advance knowledge, its direction and evaluation has to be left to innovators and users of advanced knowledge, just as the direction and evaluation of applied research has to be left to entrepreneurs and users of the things to which that research is applied. Whether such research also contributes to the solution of practical problems is a secondary consideration, just as the intrinsic intellectual contribution is a secondary matter for users in need of a solution to a practical problem.

The fact that many of the students will become applied scientists or teachers, rather than pure research workers, is immaterial. Good training of people to do advanced work in applied

[8]The term "nondirected research" is often used in the same sense as "pure research" is used here. I prefer "pure research," because research guided by intellectual concerns cannot be described as "nondirected."

research or college teaching requires more than apprenticing them to someone doing the same job. Universities are needed to overtrain most of their students (although some will become advanced research workers and thus, not overtrained) in order to give them flexibility and perspective to advance the level of their work. As has been seen in Chapter 5, successful university research has always depended on the ability of universities to select some students who do not remain in the university system, but who are interested and capable of being trained in research. The teachers who give them this kind of overtraining have to be different from competent practitioners; they have to be competent and, preferably, original thinkers and investigators in an intellectually recognized field (which, of course, also has to further the purposes of the students).

In addition to these routine needs, there is also need for the nonroutine support of pure science. One of the characteristics of science has been that some of its more important advances have been unexpected, and—in the beginning—difficult to fit into any program of study. There are also cases when the development of a new idea requires special investments that cannot be budgeted for on a routine basis. The support of such work is an essential function that requires special mechanisms.

Therefore the recommendation that universities have to make greater efforts to serve clients in research and training does not imply that they should divert their resources to practically oriented research. To serve society as universities—rather than competing with or duplicating the work of industry, parliament, or government departments—they have to be effective in their own work, namely, the creation and dissemination of advanced knowledge. Thus while they have to encourage their staff to take interest in practical problems, to do consultations, and to see whether their intellectual activities can be combined with investigating problems of interest to industry or others (preferably willing to pay for the research), their primary responsibility is to ensure that those who teach advanced students do up-to-date research of the highest quality. If they neglect this task, whatever else they do, they have neglected their primary responsibility to society.

The same conclusion applies also to governmental and private funding agencies. The idea that they have to encourage research directed to social ends, rather than pure research, is

based on the same kind of fallacy that led to the disappoint-
ments of the 1960s. Although it rejects the criterion of economic
(industrial) return, it still assumes that research will spawn
practical applications if only directed toward the right objectives. Practical applications, however, can come only from
direct contact between users and researchers, since only such
contact can help to define the characteristics of solutions for
which there is real demand so that they can be actually put to
practical use at a given time.[9] Usually, such work can be
financed by the prospective client, whether a governmental
department or a private firm. On the other hand, pure research,
especially of the nonroutine kind, requires support that can
come only from government or private foundations set up for
that purpose. Impairing the authority or dismantling the capacity of these foundations to support pure research would leave a
serious gap.

These considerations are of particular importance for the
support of science in small and medium-sized countries. European countries spent much or most of their science budgets in
the 1950s and 1960s on large-scale projects in nuclear and space
research. This was done in pursuit of a mixture of not clearly
defined military, technological, and scientific objectives, but
led to very few usable results, and many projects were discontinued after the investment of huge sums. Technological applications in these fields began to appear when industry initiated
research (Carmi, 1975). Although scientifically some of this
work was of high value, it is likely that even in this respect the
results would have been better had the money been invested in
the more balanced development of university research.

CONCLUSION According to this analysis there is no reason to assume that
general social demand for professional training, general higher
education, or research will decline in the long run. The rate of
increase of the demand has slowed down, and there is a need to
reorient research to new problems—a painful and risky process. But all this does not explain the feeling of crisis and
anomie that prevails in many academic circles. That derives
mainly from internal causes, namely, the difficulties of systems

[9]The dependence of useful inventions on demand rather than on the advancement of scientific knowledge has been shown by Schmookler (1966).

of higher education to accommodate within their existing structures their new and extended functions.

These difficulties, accompanied by the slowdown in demand, have given rise to anomie and chiliastic yearnings for "revolutionary" changes in many academic circles. Like all revolutionaries, academic ones want changes that will eliminate all present difficulties and forestall all future ones. The essence of their recommendations is to subject higher education and research to direct political control so that they serve explicit social objectives. This would—in their view—prevent such phenomena as the exaggerated growth and inevitable setback of the 1960s and the real or alleged iniquities in higher education that gave rise to so much bitterness and strife in recent years.

However, if the present analysis has been correct, such "revolutionary" changes would be a purely symptomatic treatment. No new political body, whether democratically elected or ruling as a result of seizure of power by force, is likely to have greater wisdom than the individuals and institutions actually engaged in research, teaching, and study in deciding whether pure research is good or bad for society, or what kind of general intellectual or moral education is most appropriate. Therefore, the only result of attempts to submit systems of higher education to direct political control would be greater uniformity, more bureaucratic rigidity, and more emphasis on technological goals and measurable targets. This, indeed, has been the result of the French post-Revolutionary Napoleonic reforms, as well as those of the Communist systems, all of which have been based on the principle of political control and subjection of the system to explicit considerations of social welfare. Such considerations inevitably end up in attempts to measure returns to education and research and—since this is difficult—to define returns based on whatever can be measured. It is no coincidence that the econometric and other quantitative approaches to science policy have been among the most enthusiastically adopted parts of Western social science in the Communist countries in recent years (Rabkin, 1974, 1976). Thus the revolutionary remedy would actually lead to precisely the same kind of fallacies that prevailed in the 1960s and caused so many of the present difficulties.

Therefore, what is required today is a consolidation of the fundamental changes that have occurred during the last quarter of a century. To find the means required to be able to admit up to half of the relevant age group and to train people and forge ideas and tools for the research requirements of a society in which decisions in every walk of life are increasingly based on research is the challenge faced by higher education today. No revolutionary shortcuts, but only imagination and patient work will be able to meet it.

References

Albu, Austen: "The Great Consultant and His Heritage" (review article), *Minerva*, vol. 12, no. 2, pp. 327–336, Summer 1975.

Archer, Margaret Scotford (ed.): *Students, University and Society*, Heinemann Educational Books, Ltd., London, 1972.

Armytage, W. H. G.: *Civic Universities: Aspects of a British Tradition*, Ernest Benn, Ltd., London, 1955.

Ashby, Sir Eric: *Universities: British, Indian, African: A Study in the Ecology of Higher Education*, Weidenfeld and Nicolson, London, 1966.

Ashby, Sir Eric: "The Future of the Nineteenth Century Idea of a University," *Minerva*, vol. 6, no. 1, pp. 3–17, Autumn 1967.

Atcon, Rudolf: *The Latin American University: A Key for an Integrated Approach to the Coordinated Social, Economic and Educational Development of Latin America*, ECO Revista de la Cultura de Occidente, Bogotá, 1966.

Baker, Keith Michael: *Condorcet: From Natural Philosophy to Social Mathematics*, The University of Chicago Press, Chicago, 1975.

Barbagli, Marzio: *Disoccupazione Intellectuale e Sistema Scolastico in Italia (1859–1974)*, Il Mulino, Bologna, 1974.

Bartholomew, James Richard: "The Acculturation of Science in Japan: Kitasato Shibasaburo and the Japanese Bacteriology Community, 1885–1920," unpublished Ph.D. dissertation, Stanford University, Stanford, Calif., 1971.

Baxter, James Phinney: *Scientists Against Time*, Little, Brown and Company, Boston, 1946; The M.I.T. Press, Cambridge, Mass., 1968.

Béland, Francois: "Du Paradoxe professionnel: Les Médicins et les Ingénieurs des Années 1800," *European Journal of Sociology*, forthcoming.

Bell, Daniel: "The Measurement of Knowledge and Technology," in E. B. Sheldon and W. E. Moore (eds.), *Indicators of Social Change,* Russell Sage Foundation, New York, 1968.

Ben-David, Joseph: "Professions in the Class System of Present-Day Societies," *Current Sociólogy,* vol. 12, no. 3, pp. 284–298, 1963–64.

Ben-David, Joseph: *The Scientist's Role in Society,* Prentice-Hall, Inc., Englewood Cliffs, N.J., 1971.

Ben-David, Joseph: *American Higher Education: Directions Old and New,* McGraw-Hill Book Company, New York, 1972.

Ben-David, Joseph, and Abraham Zloczower: "Universities and Academic Systems in Modern Societies," *European Journal of Sociology,* vol. 3, pp. 45–84, 1962.

Billroth, Theodor: *The Medical Sciences in the German Universities,* The Macmillan Company, New York, 1924.

Blank, David M., and George J. Stigler: *The Demand and Supply of Scientific Personnel,* National Bureau of Economic Research, Inc., New York, 1957.

Blanpied, William: "Subjective Impressions regarding Contemporary Trends," *The Ethical and Human Implications of Science and Technology,* Newsletter of the Program of Public Conceptions of Science, no. 8, pp. 136–156, June 1974.

Boffey, Philip M.: "Was There an Anti-Science Backlash?" *Science,* vol. 191, p. 1032, March 1976.

Bourricaud, François: "The French University as a 'Fixed Society,'" *Newsletter: The International Council on the Future of the University,* vol. 2, no. 4, October 1975.

Brunschwig, Henri: *Enlightenment and Romanticism in Eighteenth Century Prussia,* The University of Chicago Press, Chicago, 1974.

Burn, Barbara B.: *Higher Education in Nine Countries,* McGraw-Hill Book Company, New York, 1971.

Busch, Alexander: *Die Geschichte des Privatdozenten,* Ferdinand Enke Verlag, Stuttgart, 1959.

Bush, Vannevar: *Science, the Endless Frontier: A Report to the President,* U.S. Government Printing Office, Washington, D.C., 1945.

Bush, Vannevar: *Endless Horizons,* Public Affairs Press, Washington, D.C., 1946.

Cardwell, D. S. L.: *The Organization of Science in England: A Retrospect,* William Heinemann, Ltd., London, 1957.

Carmi, Menahem: "Shittuf Peula Bemada Vetekhnologiya Bithumei Haatom Vehehalal: Mehkar Mikre Baintegratziya Haeropith"

[European collaboration in nuclear and space research: a case study in European integration], unpublished Ph.D. dissertation, Hebrew University, Jerusalem, 1975.

Carnegie Commission on Higher Education: *New Students and New Places: Policies for the Future Growth and Development of American Higher Education*, McGraw-Hill Book Company, New York, 1971.

Carnegie Commission on Higher Education: *Reform on Campus: Changing Students, Changing Academic Programs*, McGraw-Hill Book Company, New York, 1972.

Carr-Saunders, A. M., and P. A. Wilson: *The Professions*, Oxford University Press, London, 1933.

Clark, Terry Nichols: *Prophets and Patrons: The French University and the Emergence of the Social Sciences*, Harvard University Press, Cambridge, Mass., 1973.

Coben, Stanley: "The Scientific Establishment and the Transmission of Quantum Mechanics to the United States, 1919–32," *American Historical Review*, vol. 76, no. 2, pp. 442–466, April 1971.

Cole, Jonathan R., and Stephen Cole: *Social Stratification in Science*, The University of Chicago Press, Chicago, 1973.

Commonwealth Universities Yearbook (title varies), The Association of Commonwealth Universities, London, 1936, 1952, 1962, 1973, 1974.

Conseil de l'Europe, Committee for Higher Education and Research: *Symposium on Reform and Planning of Higher Education, Oxford, 31 March–5 April 1974: Final Report*, File no. 3.1.1–2.2.2, Strasbourg, May 20, 1974. (Mimeographed.)

Crosland, Maurice: *The Society of Arcueil*, Harvard University Press, Cambridge, Mass., 1967.

Davis, James A.: *Great Aspirations: The Graduate School Plans of American College Seniors*, Aldine Publishing Company, Chicago, 1964.

Davis, James A.: *Undergraduate Career Decisions*, Aldine Publishing Company, Chicago, 1965.

Denison, Edward F.: *The Sources of Economic Growth in the U.S.*, Committee on Economic Development, New York, 1962.

Domes, Jürgen: "Current Problems in German Higher Education," *Newsletter: The International Council on the Future of the University*, vol. 3, no. 1, February 1976.

Domes, J., and A. P. Frank: "The Tribulations of the Free University of Berlin," *Minerva*, vol. 13, no. 2, pp. 183–199, Summer 1975.

Dore, Ronald R.: *Education in Tokugawa Japan*, University of California Press, Berkeley, 1965.

Duncan, Beverly: "Trends in Output and Distribution of Schooling," in E. B. Sheldon and W. E. Moore (eds.), *Indicators of Social Change*, Russell Sage Foundation, New York, 1968.

Durkheim, Emile: *Suicide*, The Free Press, Glencoe, Ill., 1951.

DuShane, Graham: "The Long Pull," *Science*, vol. 126, no. 3281, p. 997, Nov. 15, 1957.

Flexner, Abraham: *Medical Education in Europe*, Carnegie Corporation, New York, 1912.

Flexner, Abraham: *Medical Education: A Comparative Study*, Macmillan, New York, 1925.

Flexner, Abraham: *Universities: American, German, English*, Oxford University Press, New York, 1930.

Floud, Jean E., A. H. Halsey, and F. M. Martin (eds.): *Social Class and Educational Opportunity*, William Heinemann, Ltd., London, 1956.

Folger, John K., Helen S. Astin, and Alan E. Bayer: *Human Resources and Higher Education*, Russell Sage Foundation, New York, 1970.

Foster, Philip: "False and Real Problems of African Universities," *Minerva*, vol. 13, no. 3, pp. 466–478, Autumn 1975.

Freeman, C., and A. Young: *The Research and Development in Western Europe, North America and the Soviet Union: An Experimental International Comparison of Research Expenditures and Manpower in 1962*, Organisation for Economic Co-operation and Development, Paris, 1965.

Freeman, Richard B.: *The Market for College-Trained Manpower: A Study in the Economics of Career Choices*, Harvard University Press, Cambridge, Mass., 1971.

Freeman, Richard B., and David W. Breneman: *Forecasting the Ph.D. Labor Market: Pitfalls for Policy*, National Board on Graduate Education, Washington, D.C., April 1974.

Gagliardi, E.: *Die Universität Zürich 1833–1933 and ihre Verläufer*, Verlag der Erziehungsdiretion, Zurich, 1938.

Gallup, George: "The Impact of College Years: Part 2," *The Gallup Poll*, Princeton, N.J., released May 19, 1975. (6 pages.)

Gerth, H. H., and C. Wright Mills (eds.): *From Max Weber: Essays in Sociology*, Oxford University Press, New York, 1946.

Gillispie, A.: "English Ideas of the University in the 19th Century," in M. Clapp (ed.), *The Modern University*, Cornell University Press, Ithaca, N.Y., 1950.

Grimm, Tilemann: *Erziehung und Politik im konfuzianischen China der Ming Zeit (1368–1644): Mitteilungen der Gesellschaft für Natur and*

Völkerkunde Ostasiens, vol. 35B, Kommissionsverlag Otto Ha-rassowitz, Wiesbaden, Hamburg, 1960.

Gruber, W., D. Mehta, and R. Vernon: "The R&D Factor in International Trade and International Investment of United States Industries," *Journal of Political Economy,* vol. 75, no. 1, pp. 20–37, 1967.

Guerlac, Henri: "Science and French National Strength," in Edward Mead Earle (ed.), *Modern France,* Russell and Russell, New York, 1964.

Gustafson, Thane: "The Controversy over Peer Review," *Science,* vol. 190, no. 4219, pp. 1060–1066, Dec. 12, 1975.

Gustin, Bernard: "The Chemical Profession in Germany," unpublished Ph.D. dissertation, University of Chicago, Department of Sociology, 1975.

Hagstrom, Warren O.: *The Scientific Community,* Basic Books, Inc., Publishers, New York, 1965.

Hahn, Roger: *The Anatomy of a Scientific Institution: The French Academy of Sciences, 1666–1803,* University of California Press, Berkeley, 1971.

Halsey, A. H., Jean E. Floud, and C. Arnold Anderson (eds.): *Education, Economy and Society,* The Free Press of Glencoe, Inc., New York, 1961.

Halsey, H. H., and M. A. Trow: *The British Academics,* Harvard University Press, Cambridge, Mass., 1971.

Hans, Nicholas: *New Trends in Education in the Eighteenth Century,* Routledge & Kegan Paul, Ltd., London, 1951.

Harris, Seymour E.: *A Statistical Portrait of Higher Education,* McGraw-Hill Book Company, New York, 1972.

Hauser, Robert M., "Review Essay: On Boudon's Model of Social Mobility," *American Jounal of Sociology,* vol. 81, no. 4, pp. 911–928, January 1976.

Hoggart, Richard: "UNESCO in Crisis: The Israel Resolutions," *Universities Quarterly,* vol. 30, no. 1, pp. 15–23, Winter 1975.

Hutchins, Robert M.: *The Higher Learning in America,* Yale University Press, New Haven, Conn., 1936.

Irsay, Stephen D': *Històire des Universités françaises et étrangères,* Picard, Paris, 1935, vol. 2.

Jamous, H., and B. Peloille: "Professions or Self-perpetuating Systems? Changes in the French University Hospital System," in J. A. Jackson (ed.), *Professions and Professionalization,* Harvard University Press, Cambridge, Mass., 1970.

Johnson, Paul: "The Destructive Pressure of 'An Incantation of Deceiving Spirits,'" *The Times Higher Education Supplement*, Oct. 31, 1975, p. 13.

Kahl, Joseph A.: *The American Class Structure*, Rinehart & Company, Inc., New York, 1959.

Kedouri, Elie: "Arab Political Memoirs," *Encounter*, vol. 39, no. 5, pp. 70–83, November 1972.

Keesing, D. B.: "The Impact of Research and Development on United States Trade," *The Journal of Political Economy*, vol. 75, no. 1, pp. 38–48, 1967.

Kerr, Clark: *The Uses of the University*, Harvard University Press, Cambridge, Mass., 1963.

Klein, Felix: "Mathematik, Physik, Astronomie," in W. Lexis (ed.), *Die Universitäten im deutschen Reich*, Asher, Berlin, 1904, vol. 1, pp. 243–266.

Kohler, R.: "The Background to Edward Büchner's Discovery of Cell-free Fermentation," in *Journal of Historical Biology*, vol. 4, no. 1, pp. 35–61, 1971.

König, René: *Vom Wesen der deutschen Universität*, Wissenschaftliche Buchgesellschaft, Darmstadt, 1970.

Kotschnig, Walter Maria: *Unemployment in the Learned Professions*, Oxford University Press, London, 1937.

Kundt, A.: "Physik," in W. Lexis (ed.), *Die deutschen Universitäten*, Asher, Berlin, 1893, vol. 2, pp. 25–35.

Ladd, E. C., and S. M. Lipset: *The Divided Academy: Professors and Politics*, McGraw-Hill Book Company, New York, 1975.

Liard, Louis: *L'enseignement Superieur en France: 1789–1889*, Armand Colin et Cie, Editeurs, Paris, vol. 1, 1888; vol. 2, 1894.

Lipset, Seymour Martin: *The First New Nation*, Basic Books, Inc., Publishers, New York, 1963.

Lipset, Seymour Martin: *American Student Activism in Comparative Perspective*, U.S. Department of Labor, Manpower Administration, Washington, D.C., 1969.

Lipset, Seymour Martin (ed.): *Student Politics*, Basic Books, Inc., Publishers, New York, 1967.

Lipset, S. M., and S. S. Wolin: *The Berkeley Student Revolt*, Doubleday & Company, Inc., Anchor Books, Garden City, N.Y., 1965.

Lipset, S. M., et al.: "The Psychology of Voting: An Analysis of Political Behavior," in Lindzey Gardner (ed.), *Handbook of Social*

Psychology, Addison-Wesley Press, Inc., Cambridge, Mass., 1954, vol. 2, pp. 1124–1175.

McKie, Douglas: *Antoine Lavoisier: Scientist, Economist, Social Reformer,* Henry Schuman, Inc., Publishers, New York, 1952.

Mannheim, Karl: *Man and Society in an Age of Reconstruction,* Harcourt, Brace and Company, Inc., New York, 1944.

Marshall, T. H.: *Citizenship and Social Class,* Harvard University Press, Cambridge, Mass., 1950.

Merton, Robert K.: *The Sociology of Science: Theoretical and Empirical Investigations,* The University of Chicago Press, Chicago, 1973.

Mesthene, Emanuel G. (ed.): *Ministers Talk about Science,* Organisation for Economic Co-operation and Development, Paris, 1965.

National Education Association: *Teacher Supply and Demand in Universities, Colleges, and Junior Colleges, 1957–58, 1958–59,* and subsequent reports at two-year intervals, Washington, D.C., 1959, 1961, 1963, 1965.

National Science Foundation: *American Science Manpower, 1970: A Report of the National Register of Scientific and Technical Personnel,* NSF 71-45, Washington, D.C., December 1971.

National Science Foundation: *Science Indicators 1974: Report of the National Science Board, 1975,* Washington, D.C., 1976.

"News of Science," *Science,* vol. 126, no. 3277, p. 740, Oct. 18, 1957*a.*

"News of Science," *Science,* vol. 126, no. 3280, p. 965, Nov. 8, 1957*b.*

Okada, Yuzuru: "Introduction," to special issue, "Japanese Intellectuals," *Journal of Social and Political Ideas in Japan,* vol. 2, no. 1, pp. 2–7, April 1964.

Organisation for Economic Co-operation and Development: *Reviews of National Science Today—France,* Paris, 1966.

Organisation for Economic Co-operation and Development: *The Overall Level and Structure of R&D Efforts in OECD Member Countries,* Paris, 1967*a.*

Organisation for Economic Co-operation and Development: *Reviews of National Science Policy: United Kingdom and Germany,* Paris, 1967*b.*

Organisation for Economic Co-operation and Development: *Reviews of National Science Policy: United States,* Paris, 1968.

Organisation for Economic Co-operation and Development: *Innovation in Higher Education: Reforms in Yugoslavia,* Paris, 1970.

Organisation for Economic Co-operation and Development: *Development of Higher Education 1950–1965: Analytical Report,* Paris, 1971.

Organisation for Economic Co-operation and Development, Centre for Educational Research and Innovation (CERI): *Interdisciplinarity: Problems of Teaching and Research in Universities,* n.p., 1972.

Organisation for Economic Co-operation and Development: *The Research System,* Paris, 1973, vol. 2.

Organisation for Economic Co-operation and Development: *The Research System,* Paris, 1974*a,* vol. 3 (Canada, United States, Conclusions).

Organisation for Economic Co-operation and Development: *Structure of Studies and Place of Research in Mass Higher Education,* Paris, 1974*b.*

Organisation for Economic Co-operation and Development: *Towards Mass Higher Education: Issues and Dilemmas,* Paris, 1974*c.*

Orlans, Harold: *The Effect of Federal Programs on Higher Education: A Study of 36 Universities and Colleges,* The Brookings Institution, Washington, D.C., 1962.

Orlans, Harold (ed.): *Science, Policy and the University,* The Brookings Institution, Washington, D.C., 1968.

Parsons, Talcott: "Age and Sex in the Social Structure of the United States (1942)," *Essays on Sociological Theory,* The Free Press, Glencoe, Ill., 1949; rev. ed., 1954.

Paulsen, Friedrich: *Geschichte des Gelehrten Unterrichts,* Verlag von Veite Company, Leipzig, 1897, vol. 2; 3d ed., Walter de Gruyter and Co., Berlin, 1921.

Paulsen, Friedrich: *Die deutschen Universitäten und das Universitätstudium,* 1902; reprint ed., Georg Olms Verlags Buchhandlung, Hildesheim, 1966.

Peterson, Richard E., and John A. Bilorusky: *May 1970: The Campus Aftermath of Cambodia and Kent State,* Carnegie Commission on Higher Education, Berkeley, Calif., 1971.

Piobetta, J. B.: *Les Institutions Universitaires en France,* Presses Universitaires de France, Paris, 1951.

Pipes, Richard: "The Historical Evolution of the Russian Intelligentsia," *The Russian Intelligentsia,* Columbia University Press, New York, 1961.

Poignant, Raymond: *Education and Development in Western Europe, the United States, and the U.S.S.R.: A Comparative Study,* Teachers College Press, Columbia University, New York, 1969.

Price, Derek J. de Solla: *Little Science, Big Science,* Columbia University Press, New York, 1963.

Probstein, R. F.: "Reconversion and Academic Research," in Allen Jonathan (ed.), *March 4: Scientists, Students, and Society*, The M.I.T. Press, Cambridge, Mass., 1970.

Prost, Antoine: *Histoire de l'Enseignement en France: 1800–1967*, Librairie Armand Colin, Paris, 1968.

Purver, Margery: *The Royal Society: Concept and Creation*, Routledge & Kegan Paul, London, 1967.

Psacharopoulos, G., assisted by Keith Hinchliffe: *Returns to Education: An International Comparison*, Jossey-Bass Inc., Publishers, San Francisco, 1973.

Rabkin, Y. M.: "Origines et développement de la recherche sur la recherche en Union Soviétique," *Le Progrès Scientifique*, vol. 170, pp. 39–51, 1974.

Rabkin, Y. M.: "Naukometricheskie issledovania v khmii [Scientometric Studies in Chemistry]. Moskva: izd, Moskogovskogo Universiteta, 1974, 136 pp., 33 kop," (review article), *Social Studies of Science*, vol. 6, no. 1, pp. 128–132, February 1976.

Reader, William Joseph: *Professional Men: The Rise of the Professional Classes in Nineteenth Century England*, Basic Books, Inc., Publishers, New York, 1966.

Ringer, Fritz: *The Decline of the German Mandarins: The German Academic Community, 1890–1933*, Harvard University Press, Cambridge, Mass., 1969.

Roszak, Theodore: "The Monster and the Tital: Science, Knowledge and Gnosis," *Daedalus*, vol. 103, no. 3, pp. 17–32, Summer 1974.

Rueschemeyer, Dietrich: *Lawyers and their Society*, Harvard University Press, Cambridge, Mass., 1973.

Sanderson, Michael: *The Universities and British Industry, 1850–1970*, Routledge & Kegan Paul, London, 1972.

Schmookler, Jacob: *Invention and Economic Growth*, Harvard University Press, Cambridge, Mass., 1966.

Schnabel, Franz: *Deutsche Geschichte im neunzehnten Jahrhundert*, Verlag Herder, Freiburg, 1959, vol. 1, vol. 3.

Schumpeter, Joseph A.: *Capitalism, Socialism and Democracy*, Harper & Brothers, New York, 1947.

Sekine, Thomas T.: "Uno-Riron: A Japanese Contribution to Marxian Political Economy," *Journal of Economic Literature*, vol. 13, no. 3, pp. 847–877, September 1975.

Sewell, William H., and Vinnal P. Shah: "Socioeconomic Status, Intelligence and the Attainment of Higher Education," *Sociology of Education,* vol. 40, no. 1, pp. 1–23, Winter 1967.

Shils, Edward: "Authoritarianism: 'Right' and 'Left,'" in R. Christie and M. Jahoda (eds.), *Studies in the Scope and Method of the Authoritarian Personality,* The Free Press, Glencoe, Ill., 1954.

Shils, Edward: "The Implantation of Universities: Reflections on a Theme of Ashby," *Universities Quarterly,* vol. 22, no. 2, pp. 142–166, Spring 1966.

Shils, Edward: "The Intellectuals and the Future," and "Plenitude and Scarcity: The Anatomy of an International Cultural Crisis," *The Intellectuals and the Powers,* The University of Chicago Press, Chicago, 1972.

Shimbori, Michiya: "Zengakuren: A Japanese Case Study of a Student Political Movement," in *Sociology of Education,* vol. 37, no. 3, pp. 229–253, Spring 1964.

Shimbori, Michiya: "The Sociology of a Student Movement: A Japanese Case Study," *Daedalus,* vol. 97, no. 1, pp. 204–228, Winter 1968.

Shimbori, Michiya: "Comparison Between Pre- and Post-War Student Movements in Japan," *Sociology of Education,* vol. 37, no. 1, pp. 59–70, Fall 1973.

Silvert, Kalman H.: "The University Student," in John J. Johnson (ed.), *Continuity and Change in Latin America,* Stanford University Press, Stanford, Calif., 1964.

Sloan, Douglas: *The Scottish Enlightenment and the American College Ideal,* Teachers College Press, Columbia University, New York, 1971.

Spurr, Stephen: *Academic Degree Structures: Innovative Approaches,* McGraw-Hill Book Company, New York, 1970.

Stinchcombe, Arthur L.: "Some Empirical Consequences of the Davis-Moore Theory of Stratification (1963)," in Reinhard Bendix and Seymour Martin Lipset (eds.), *Class, Status and Power,* 2d ed., The Free Press, New York, 1966.

Taton, René (ed.): *Enseignement et diffusion des sciences en France au XVIIIᵉ siècle,* Hermann & Cie, Paris, 1964.

Trow, Martin: *Problems in the Transition from Elite to Mass Higher Education,* paper prepared for a conference on mass higher education held by the Organisation for Economic Co-operation and Development in Paris in June 1973.

Truscot, Bruce: *Redbrick University,* Faber & Faber, Ltd., London, 1943.

U.S. Bureau of the Census: *Statistical Abstract of the United States,* 1957, 1967, 1972.

U.S. Office of Education: *Earned Degrees Conferred by Higher Educational Institutions*, no. 262, November 1949.

U.S. Office of Education: *Earned Degrees Conferred by Higher Educational Institutions*, no. 570, May 1959.

U.S. Office of Education: *Earned Degrees Conferred: 1967–68, Part A—Summary Data*, 1969.

U.S. Office of Education: *Earned Degrees Conferred: 1970–71*, 1973.

Ushiogi, Morikazu: "A Comparative Study of the Occupational Structure of University Graduates," *The Developing Economies*, vol. 9, no. 3, pp. 350–368, September 1971.

Ushiogi, Morikazu: "The Japanese Student and the Labor Market," n.p., n.p., 1976. (Mimeographed.)

Veysey, Laurence R.: *The Emergence of the American University*, The University of Chicago Press, Chicago, 1965.

Weber, Max: *From Max Weber: Essays in Sociology*, ed. H. H. Gerth and C. Wright Mills, Kegan Paul, Trench, Trubner & Co., Ltd., London, 1947.

Weinberg, M. Alvin: *Reflections on Big Science*, The M.I.T. Press, Cambridge, Mass., 1967.

Worms, Jean-Pierre: "The French Student Movement," in Seymour Martin Lipset (ed.), *Student Politics*, Basic Books, Inc., Publishers, New York, 1967.

Worthington, Peter: "The Secret Czech Report," *The Toronto Sun*, Nov. 25, 1975, p. 11.

Yesufu, T. M. (ed.): *Creating the African University: Emerging Issues of the 70's*, Oxford University Press, Ibadan and London, 1973.

Yuasa, Mitsutomo: "The Shifting Center of Scientific Activity in the West: From the 16th to the 20th Century," in Shigeru Nakayama, David L. Swain, and Yagi Eri (eds.), *Science and Society in Modern Japan*, pp. 81–103, The M.I.T. Press, Cambridge, Mass., 1974.

Zeldin, Theodore: "Higher Education in France, 1848–1940," *Journal of Contemporary History*, vol. 2, no. 3, pp. 53–80, 1967.

Zloczower, A.: *Career Opportunities and the Growth of Scientific Discovery in 19th Century Germany* (with special reference to physiology), Occasional Papers in Sociology, the Hebrew University of Jerusalem, 1966.

Index

DATE DUE